The Mysticism of Emma Curtis Hopkins

Volume I

Realizing the Christ Within

The Mysticism of Emma Curtis Hopkins

Volume I

Realizing the Christ Within

Note: There are no or very few references in Emma's writings. With my background rooted in the Christian Scriptures, I have prayerfully included any Bible references I could find. There are many quotations from other Sacred Texts like the Bhagavad Gita, or the Upanishads for example. In time students will identify other references that will give credit to any original writings by which Emma might have been inspired. The teachings are universal and helpful to people of all walks of life. Emma Curtis Hopkins' writings are in Public Domain - any copyright on *The Mysticism of Emma Curtis Hopkins* is for the distillation and arrangement of the original materials. Emma's words are timeless and precious many of her books are published by Wise Woman Press, Desert Church of the Learning Light and by the Emma Curtis Hopkins Theological Association.

Volume I – Realizing the Christ Within

Compiled by Ute Maria Cedilla

© Ministry of the Highwatch 2013

Managing Editor: Michael Terranova

ISBN: 978-0945385-47-9

WiseWoman Press

Vancouver, WA 98665

www.wisewomanpress.com

www.emmacurtishopkins.com

Contents

Foreword xi

Introduction xv

    The Message of Emma Curtis Hopkins xv

    Tribute xviii

    Excerpts from "The Baccalauréat Address" of 1891 xx

    Covenant xxiii

    The Twelve Gates xxv

Chapter One – The Silent Edict 1

Chapter Two – Remission, Denial of all but God 17

Chapter Three – Forgiveness, Affirmation of all as God 29

Chapter Four – Faith, the Evidence that God is All 47

Chapter Five – Works are the rest of mind in the Presence of God 65

Chapter Six – Understanding of God 87

The Radiant "I AM" 109

Class Notes 116

    Chapter One - The Silent Edict 116

    Chapter Two - Remission, Denial of all but God. 119

    Chapter Three - Forgiveness, Affirmation of all as God. 122

    Chapter Four - Faith, the Evidence that God is All. 125

    Chapter Five - Works are the rest of mind in the Presence of God 128

    Chapter Six - Understanding of God, the only understanding worthwhile. 131

Foreword

In the late 1980s I "rescued" two slightly damaged books that were sitting on a dusty bookshelf. As it turns out, they rescued me! One was *Scientific Christian Mental Practice*, the other *High Mysticism* by Emma Curtis Hopkins. Scientific changed my life! It was relatively easy to read, well organized and offered practical advice. Then I tried to "read" High Mysticism – little did I know that it would take years for me to even touch the hem of the garment that was hidden in Emma's mystical writings.

In the introduction of the latest Emma Biography, *"Emma Curtis Hopkins, An Appreciation for Her Students,"* Rev. Joanna Rogers points out that Emma's teachings are not to be taken out of context or out of order. Whereas I totally agree, and highly recommend her book for anyone who wishes to learn more about Emma, my personal guidance was to study High Mysticism. I was hoping that the result would be a better understanding of all the preceding works. I learn best by creating an outline of a book and so *The Mysticism of Emma Curtis Hopkins* was born. It was simply my own way of studying. For me the choice was to follow my own inner passion and guidance or leave the book on the shelf to gather more dust.

It is said that when the student is ready, the teacher appears. In my case the teacher appeared in various synchronistic events. I found a whole stack of Emma Curtis Hopkins' manuscripts published by *Highwatch Fellowship*. They were pages upon pages obviously typed on a typewriter before the days of computers. These writings were so precious to me, that I decided to preserve them in electronic format and began to type.

My experience was unexpected and rather startling. It felt as if I was in another dimension while typing Emma's words. Everything was crystal clear and made perfect sense at that moment – but in the following days the clarity was lost. The teachings were entering my sub-conscious mind and became part of me at a deep level of consciousness. Many Emma students have experienced this and acknowledge that there is a definite transference of consciousness that comes through the teachings of Emma Curtis Hopkins. This is why we call her the "Teacher of Teachers," and make every effort to keep her words intact because of their mystical power or vibration.

Another synchronistic event was meeting the Rev. Marge Flotron in Chicago. She was living, breathing and teaching Emma and had preserved and privately published any writings she could find. It was Rev. Marge who pointed out that Emma's teachings contained an evolution from the mental, to the mystical and finally to the absolute sciences. All of Emma's writings were based on the Twelve Gates which represent an evolution of consciousness at higher and higher levels. It is then that I knew that one could not just "read" Emma. Her writings have to be appropriated and must become a part of our being.

My outline of High Mysticism became my daily spiritual practice. I recorded it on cassette and listened to the text over and over. I can honestly say that my life is better with Emma. In some wonderful way, the teachings awaken the Creative Genius within. The result of studying with the Teacher of Teachers is a deeper, wider and broader connection with the One. Emma teaches me how to stand in my power and how to live from inside out.

My compilation of High Mysticism, the Twelve Gates and Résumé, is divided into two books. The first volume is dedicated to the realization of the Christ within and is based on the first six Gates or Chapters. It is fitting to end these lessons with the famous treatment *The Radiant I Am*. The second volume teaches ministry. Although Emma did not name these chapters in *High Mysticism*, I have chosen to use titles that reflect Gates seven though twelve. In my opinion *Self Treatment* is a recap of the whole teachings and belongs at the end of the second Volume. Finally, Emma teaches that describing God is a treatment in itself. I have chosen 72 names out of many more to conclude my compilation *The Mysticism of Emma Curtis Hopkins*.

Each volume contains class notes for teachers who wish to initiate a discussion group. I have only used Emma's words and have not added my opinion, which would only limit the possibilities of interpretation.

ABOUT HIGH MYSTICISM

In Studies in High Mysticism, Emma moves to the realization that there is nothing to heal, as all is already accomplished in God and that all we have to do is to recognize it.

Originally published in 1892 in twelve separate small volumes, Studies in High Mysticism was later combined into one book. The text had been extensively edited by Elizabeth Bogart, Myrtle Fillmore's secretary, before publication by DeVorss under the title of High Mysticism.

The original unedited text is now available from The Desert Church (Rev. Joanna P. Rogers) and Wise Woman Press (Michael Terranova). Rev. Rogers has also included a new Index and Addendum for her publication of Studies in High Mysticism.

Foreword

Emma always teaches in twelve lessons or Gates. She explains her chapter layouts and her reasons in *The Judgment Series*, which is undated. Here is what she writes:

"The first six lessons always deal with the divine ego whose throne is in the myself of each man. The last six lessons always deal with the divine ego in the universe whose throne is everywhere equally present.

The first lesson in Spiritual Science is called The Word. The second lesson is called Denial. The third lesson is called Affirmation. The fourth lesson is called Faith. The fifth lesson is called Works. The sixth lesson is called Understanding. The seventh is called Inheritance. The eighth is called Truth. The ninth is called Holiness. The tenth is called Forgiveness. The eleventh is called Wisdom. The twelfth is called Free Grace.

These names of the twelve lessons are modified somewhat, or changed enough to put in different terms through the metaphysical books of every age. They may all be summed up in one word. This word is the Tree of Life to him that can pick it out of the combined twelve."

Although Emma divides the Tree of Life or the Tree of Science into twelve signs she always refers back to the Soul or Spirit of humanity, looking to God as the supply for the totality of the All.

"There is one fruit we call life, another we call health, another strength, another prosperity, another protection, another is mind, another speech, another is writing, another is singing another is judgment, another is praise." Only eleven are listed in the Judgment Series. The Radiant I Am treatment includes "skill."

These studies comprised the Theological Course that ministerial students had to take. At the end of each class Emma wrote a personal *Résumé* for each student. One version was preserved and is available from Wise Woman Press. Each chapter of High Mysticism is summed up in *Résumé*, and also adds a practical application. This is the reason I have included *Résumé* at the end of each chapter of my compilation: *The Mysticism of Emma Curtis Hopkins*.

Finally, it is important to understand how Emma Curtis Hopkins interpreted the name of Jesus Christ. She explains it as follows in her Judgment Series: *"The healing power in this universe was once given the name 'Jesus Christ.' Is not that as good a name as 'God'? Suppose the adepts of the Orient can charge a name with such energy that whenever it is spoken, a miracle is wrought. They have, in times past so charged certain names. This is the case with the Name 'Jesus Christ.' One came who so filled His own Name with His omnipotent faith, that it is His own healing power, prospering power, wisdom power, to this day. He called the omnipotent Spark that shines in all men, by His own Name….*

Take that text for a fact. Take that Spark of Divinity that shines in you and call it the Jesus Christ in you. Tell it what you want done. Tell it what you want the God in the universe to perform for you. Call it by its rightful Name. Call again. Call firmly. You are speaking to the Omnipotent Spark in your being. It will force you to feel confidence, as a magnet forces a steel needle to be magnetic. And your confidence may be so absolute that you are no longer among us as human, but are present all Divine. You have faith in God. You have the faith of God."

The teachings of Emma Curtis Hopkins are universal and interfaith. They highlight the Golden Thread of Truth that is interwoven through all authentic experience of the One we call God.

And from Emma's Bible Lesson dated April 29, 1894 I quote: "From India, with her One Point, whose name is Brahman; from Arabia, with her One Presence, whose name is Allah; from Egypt, with her Father-Mother Nourisher of all, whose name is Osiris-Isis; from Persia with her Shining Light whose name is Ormuzed (or Oromasdes, the Grecianized form of the Zoroastrian deity, Ahura-Mazda); from Palestine, with her everlasting Word, which is God; we get the same scientific calculation: in that day shall the God of harmony set up a kingdom which shall consume all other kingdoms."

With deepest gratitude to the One

Ute Maria Cedilla, LUT R.Sc.P

June 3rd, 2013

Introduction

The Message of Emma Curtis Hopkins

During the many years of the active ministry of Emma Curtis Hopkins, over fifty thousand individuals came to her for instruction. Numbered among them were ministers, priests, lawyers, physicians, artists, business men and people from every walk of life.

She was known as the "Teacher of Teachers" as so many of her students later became teachers and carried the message of the High Watch to the far corners of the earth. Several of the well known schools of advanced thought in this country were founded by her students.

It is said that the glory of her teaching is that it arouses the hidden creative genius in the students so that they go forth inspired to accomplish some great work of a unique and inimitable sort by the recognition of their own inherent divinity.

The Studies in High Mysticism contain her latest writings, the full bloom of her spiritual unfoldment. They are acknowledged to be among the finest examples of Mystical writings. Mrs. Hopkins was herself a Mystic, a Mystic of a new type. She sang the song of Life triumphant over loss, pain, sickness, poverty, sin and death, and the joy that comes from living the Christ Life. Here we have no identifying with suffering and grief, but the fuller doctrine of Jesus Christ - the rise from ignorance to the "Liberty of the Children of God!" The bringing forth of this type, spiritually bold and executive is the fruition toward which all religions and philosophies are bent.

She re-states the teaching of the "Sages of the Ages" whereby the earnest students may find God in the inmost sanctuary of their being, "for truly the Highest is the Nearest, Most Distant yet Most Present, and we are in His image." "The Highest and the Inmost God is one God."

She tells us that, "The Sacred Books of all ages mention three Sciences: Material, Mental and Mystical. Material Science declares laws that are sure: as iron sharpens iron, and hydrogen and oxygen clashing together fall into thirst-quenching water.

"The Sacred Books proclaim a Mental Science to which the world can subscribe, as 'All that we are is made up of our thought.'

Introduction

"Mystical Science announces the miracles of 'Predicate-less Being,' setting the ways of matter at nought, and nullifying the thought of the mind:

"The flesh profiteth nothing.'

"Take no thought.'

"In such a moment as ye think not."

Mystical Science is the chalice of golden wine passed along to the sons of men by John's angels of the Apocalypse. It is a new song for the hearts of the children of the New Age.

The Mystical Science is the oldest Science in the world. It concerns that swift, subtle faculty possessed by us all, whereby we look whithersoever we will; to the Deity ever beholding us, or to the dust beneath without the aid of our physical eyes.

"Thou canst not behold me with thy two outer eyes: I have given thee an eye divine."

The Divine Eye or Vision, is the sense with which we perceive Truth or Reality. "This faculty, swifter that the fleetest thought, being rested steadfastly upon any given point, can bring back to the waiting mind all the facts that pertain to the resting place. It is the lifting up of this sense out of the network of materiality, the wheel of incessant grind, that takes us above our disasters and difficulties.

"We are all harvesting according to our inward viewings. 'Why are we troubled?' "We always look toward an object before thinking it, and it is by having oft recourse to inward viewing that then the mind goes on to know and comprehend."

Therefore, "Vision often Godward and live anew. So shall the body be like 'a tree planted by rivers of water, whose leaf fadeth not.' Vision often Godward so that affairs also may go well. Gaze often toward Our Father, and all thoughts shall be like morning music. Lift up an inward look now and then to a country whose ether winds every raying forth their healing aura, are swift remedies for all the world's unhappiness."

Introduction

The one volume edition of the "Twelve Studies in High Mysticism fulfills a purpose stated by Mrs. Hopkins in one of the very early printings of the Second Study, "In due time all the twelve lessons will appear in one book."

A companion book to "*High Mysticism*" is "*Résumé,*" a practice book for the twelve studies.

Introduction

Tribute

Like so many others among the teachers and students of the new spiritual teaching, she sought freedom from illness in Christian Science, then in its infancy. Emma Curtis Hopkins studied with Mrs. Mary Baker Eddy for two years. Then going out as an independent teacher, she taught in many cities - New York, Chicago, Kansas City, San Francisco, with large classes wherever she went.

Emma Curtis Hopkins had a broad education and was familiar with the Hebrew Scriptures, the Vedas, the Bhagavad-Gita and other sacred writings of India. She also studied the philosophy and mysteries of the Greeks, such as Orpheus, Pythagoras, Plato, and Plotinus. Having learned Greek at an early age, she read many of these in the original language. She had an exhaustive knowledge of the histories of all nations and peoples of all times. Her Biblical interpretations are masterpieces.

Returning to Chicago, she established a school for the teaching of the philosophy now called Spiritual Science, Divine Science, and New Thought.

In 1888, Mrs. Hopkins founded a seminary in Chicago, which she called: *The Christian Science Theological Seminary*. It was a regular incorporated school and the graduates were ordained ministers and so recognized by the State of Illinois. This school was not associated with Mary Baker Eddy and Christian Science. It was in operation until 1893.

Many movements, each having its own distinctive expression, sprang from its roots. To name a few: Unity School of Christianity, Home of Truth Movement, Divine Science, and Religious Science.

Among some 50,000 students taught by Emma Curtis Hopkins, the most famous are: Charles Fillmore, Myrtle Fillmore, Ernest Holmes, H. Emilie Cady, Lillian De Waters, Frances Foulks, H.B. Jeffery, Annie Rix Militz and Marie S. Watts.

In 1893 the class register numbered 350 names of people who had received the basic lessons, and an ordained ministry numbering 111 who had received the advanced *Theological Course*.

Mrs. Hopkins was herself a genuine mystic and in all her teachings emphasized the mystic experience. Mysticism is the most difficult of all metaphysical themes, for it involves an experience rarely realized and never adequately expressed in words –

Introduction

the realization of identity with the Absolute Being, or the here and now experience of *union with God*. Mrs. Hopkins taught that the first step in developing the consciousness of the mystic was turning the attention away from all things, events, and persons toward the Deity ever beholding us.

It is said that the glory of her teaching is that it arouses the hidden creative genius in the students. This is how they went forth inspired to accomplish some great work of a unique and inimitable sort, by the recognition of their own inherent divinity. To awaken this Divine Sense in her readers is the chief aim of the writings, which she has left with us.

None of Emma Curtis Hopkins' students ever *studied* with her, for she offered no debate. What she said was it and that was that. But she empowered it with something alive, animated and inspiring. Thus, the value of her teaching was that she imparted spiritual conviction in such a way as to awaken a corresponding consciousness in her students, which she knew was already there, merely awaiting such arousal.

During the last days of her life she lived in New York City and taught only privately. It is estimated that during her active lifetime as many as fifty thousand persons came to her for instruction, either in class or privately.

Introduction

Excerpts from "The Baccalauréat Address" of 1891

Given by Emma Curtis Hopkins for an ordination in Chicago in 1891.

It has always been accorded by the wise that the baptism of the Holy Spirit, or the quickening influence of the Principle of Divine Intelligence, is the test of those called to teach the words and will of the Supreme of the universe. Those so called have not needed to quote authorities or precedents for their actions or teachings. They have all spoken as having authority. They have all come as messengers of goodness and freedom.

When the divinely appointed Jesus came, He dared to claim wisdom from the Most High Intelligence. They were amazed at His doctrine because He taught as one vested with authority. Like all the inspired who had preceded Him, He proved Himself God-sent by doing God-like works.

The suns, which had daily set upon crowds of sick and miserable people, arose at morning time to overlook joyous multitudes, healed by the divine minister of the Gospel of health. The wicked turned from the error of their ways. The mad and despairing smiled and were at peace. The poor were helped and fed. "The words that I speak unto you it is not I that speak, but the Father that dwelleth in me. He doeth the works." (John 14:10)

Jesus' example has been the inspiration and direction of millions since His time. They have all heard the voice of the Spirit and felt the impulse of goodness stirring them to go forth to help the world. Their hearts, being moved in compassion, declare a new and true world in which the poor may be taught and befriended. Where women walk fearless and glad, and where children are safe and free. Every fiber and thread of their being, every instant of their time is absolutely dedicated to the prophesied new dispensation of the Holy Spirit, with its Ministry of healing from every ill known in the old times.

They preach the powerlessness of evil and the unreality of the material universe. They declaim against the necessity for evil in any form of sin, sickness, or death. They declare the Omnipresence of God, the Good, and deny the presence or working power of any other principle but the Good. They demonstrate that the denial of evil, as a reality or working principle, puts evil into the nothingness from whence it sprang. They are putting all forms of evil completely out of and away from their life experience, when they deal with the Principle of Goodness, the only Reality.

Introduction

They are proving daily what was the teaching of Christ and His immediate followers by new interpretations of His words and imitation of His works. They urge that the misinterpretations of His teachings are accountable for all the pain and suffering and wickedness believed in by all humankind since His beautiful lifetime, when the multitude rejoiced in health and peace wherever He walked among them.

These people are the apostles of a new dispensation. They usher in the dawn of a new time when evil shall be known no more among us, because Christ, the Truth, has come again in the way of His perfect doctrine revealed anew to the waiting world. They have for their rallying cry: "Not by might, nor by strength, but by My Spirit saith the Lord," (Zech 4:6) which was the watchword of the inspired prophets of old.

We, of the new dispensation, ask the world, which is to be our church, to turn and listen to our preaching. It is the quickening message from the Supreme of the universe announcing the second coming, long expected when every mountain of trouble shall be removed, and every hill of difficulty obliterated.

Pride cannot hold its own where the spiritually taught are speaking, and learning cannot defeat the wisdom of the children of Divine Science. Listen, for we will speak of excellent things, and the opening of our lips shall be right things. We shall heed to Paul's injunction "Let us give ourselves to the ministry of the Word." (Acts 6:4)

Ministers, you are sent forth to the world that waits for the healing benediction of the Spirit with which you have been baptized. You have been tried and not found wanting. You have been called and been answered by that fullness of power by which the devout in all ages have prayed. You can heal the sick by the word of your speaking. You can cheer the fainting. "When hearts are cast down you shall say, There is lifting up." (Job 22:29) You are the revival of the full ministry of the times of old. The Lord himself shall guide you continually, and you shall want for no good thing. Speak the word boldly that is given you to utter.

For this is the faith of the fathers,

The faith the apostles delivered.

Introduction

"Now therefore go, said the voice of the Lord to Moses, and I will be with thy mouth and teach thee what thou shalt say." (Exodus 4:15)

Covenant

"Make your covenant with the Spirit, and do nothing but trust it entirely. Spirit does all things, we agree to leave ourselves entirely in its keeping." I hereby covenant with the Holy Spirit for my life, and I will do nothing to preserve my life; my life is the life of the Spirit.

I covenant with the Holy Spirit for my health; and I will do nothing to preserve my health; my health is the health of the Spirit.

I covenant with the Holy Spirit for my strength; and I will do nothing for my strength, my strength is the strength of the Spirit.

I covenant with Spirit for my support, and I will do nothing for my support; my support is the providence of the Spirit.

I covenant with the Holy Spirit for my defense, and I will do nothing for my defense; my defense is the protection of the Holy Spirit.

I covenant with the Spirit for my mind in its perfect thinking, and I will do nothing for my thoughts; my mind is the mind of the Spirit.

I covenant with the Spirit for my right speech, and I will do nothing for my speech; my speech is the voice of the Spirit.

I will do nothing to fix, or record, or write my Truth unto the earth, for my record is the record of the Holy Spirit. I say, as Job said, my witness is in the heavens and my record is on high.

I covenant for my joyous song of life, and will do nothing to be joyful; my joy is the joy of the spirit.

I covenant with the Holy Spirit for my demonstrations of efficiency and skill in rightly doing all things, and I will do nothing to perfect myself. My efficiency is the working skill of the Holy Spirit, according to the words of Jesus Christ, who said, "The words that I speak unto you I speak not of myself: but the Father that dewelleth in me, he doeth the works."

Introduction

I covenant for my judgment in its beauty, and the beauty of judgment; and I will do nothing to make myself greatly good in judgment; for the Spirit is my judgment.

I covenant with the Holy Spirit for my love, and will do nothing to make myself loving or beloved, for all is the Holy Spirit now acting with irresistible goodness through me.

This will make it easy for me to say, from the depths of my heart, "I do believe that the true God is now working with me and through me and by me and for me, to make me omnipotent, omnipresent, and omniscient. I have faith in God. I have the faith of God."

Introduction

The Twelve Gates

"Open ye the gates," said Isaiah. He meant open your mind to speak boldly the twelve words of science.

The twelve gates of revelation and prophecy and science are the twelve knowledges you already possess. The moment you hear from the roar of without, the words that are not true, you begin to close your gates. Open the twelve gates boldly. Swing open the gates of that wonderful wisdom given you from the foundation of the world. Regard nobody's teaching who believes in the power of evil. Avoid books that describe evil. Ignore people who believe in evil. Open wide the twelve gates of your noble city and shed abroad the glory of health, strength, joy, prosperity.

Do you know the twelve laws that are shut up within your wonderful mind? You had better hear them spoken boldly by somebody who knows them and believes in them, but I will give them briefly for you to speak either silently or audibly.

Remember that what you think is a wave of light going through the mental atmosphere of the world, and wherever your true thought strikes, somebody will be lifted off a bed of pain or healed of some sorrow.

There is good for me. My good is my God my life, my truth, my love, my substance, my intelligence, omnipresent, omnipotent, omniscient.

There is no mixture of evil in my good. There is no opposition to my God as material conditions of any kind. There is no absence of life, substance, intelligence. There is nothing to hate. There is no presence of sin, sickness, or death in my world, where God is the only presence and power and wisdom.

God is all. God is the omnipresent, omnipotent, omniscient good, as life, truth, love, substance, intelligence. I am my own idea of God, and I live and move and have my being according to my idea of God. I am spirit, mind, like my God, and shed abroad wisdom, strength, holiness. My God works through me to will and to do that which ought to be done by me. I am governed by the true God and am kept from sin, from suffering for sin, and I cannot fear sin, sickness or death.

I do believe that the true God is now working with me and through me and by me and for me, to make me a living demonstration of omnipresent, omnipotent, omniscient goodness.

Introduction

As spirit, I can preach the gospel, heal the sick, cast out demons, raise the dead.

I understand the secret of instantaneous spiritual demonstration.

I hold no accusations against the people of God. I do not believe in lustful passions or sensual appetites. I believe that all these are the hunger and thirst after righteousness, given a false name.

I do not accuse the people of God of deceiving each other or of being deceived. There is no opposition to truth.

I do not accuse the people of God of being sinners. It is true that all things were made by the true God and are now very good.

I do not believe in a mixture of good and evil in the universe. I stand to my confidence that all is good. All is good in truth. According to my faith so it is now unto me and unto those about me.

I cannot admit that there is any foolishness or ignorance or weakness or old age failure in omnipresent, omnipotent, omniscience. There is but one mind, and that is God - one substance and that is God.

The white soul of every creature stands out ransomed from sin, death and sorrow by the words of truth. The whole world is awake to righteousness. Time is no more. All is well now.

Judging not after the sight of the eyes nor after the hearing of the ears, these twelve gates will open and you will surely see things as they are and not as has been believed they are.

To live and think these thoughts is to shine as the sun with love and wisdom. This was the truth as lived by Jesus Christ. This is the truth Jesus Christ lives. This is the truth everlasting.

High over all principalities and powers of unbelief in the allness of God, high over all memories of your past, high out of reach of your fears of the future, live and reign in truth with Jesus Christ in you and with you and by you and for you.

Introduction

Do you not know that this truth is Jesus Christ in you? Do you not know that when you speak this truth it is Jesus Christ opening the gates of glory for your world? We rise in the triumph of knowing that the kingdom of God is within us all now.

Chapter One – The Silent Edict

Monday, First Week

1st Gate - There is Good for me. My Good is my God my Life, my Truth, my Love, my Substance, my Intelligence, Omnipresent, Omnipotent, Omniscient.

Consider now with me in joyful amazement the unity of discovery throughout the centuries, which the illuminati have made, as to that practice of the presence of Deity most surely leading to divine imbuement.

"Look unto Me and be ye saved, all the ends of the earth! For I am God and there is no other." (Is 45:22) This is a clear instruction that runs in almost verbatim language through all the sacred or charmed books of the world. It is the supreme science. Whoever can read its supernal lines, undisturbed by their company of errors, is in the way of salvation. It is that swift, subtle faculty possessed by us all, whereby we look by our own choice, to the Deity ever beholding us, or to the dust beneath, without the aid of our physical eyes. "Thou canst not behold me with thy two outer eyes, I have given thee an eye divine." *Upanishads*

This swift, subtle sense is our incorporeal eye. It is the one faculty of our immortal soul which we continually make use of. The exaltation or the lifting up of this sense toward that vast, vast Countenance ever shining toward us as the sun, is our way of return to the Source from which we came. It is the Path of Light.

Humans alone of all the animals go in quest of their Origin, and perceiving that the highest good is to be sought by them in the highest place, they look to their Maker.

This looking faculty antedates mind, and though offering itself to the service of mind, transcends it in achieving power. For it is primarily what we most see, and not what we most think, that constitutes our presence, power and history. It is not possible for anything to take place save in connection with an onlooker.

If we exalt this swift sense, or look unto Him whose ever-repeated mandate is, "Behold Me, behold Me," (Is 65:1) we receive back over the track of our vision tonic and viability to the mind. We also receive endurance and beauty to the body, joy and fearlessness to the emotions, integrity and poise to the moral character.

Chapter One – The Silent Edict

What you see is what you are. We collect sadness and depression from directing this mystic eye toward human faces. Sanity and soundness are the characteristics of the mind of those who do not project their prejudiced vision toward objects that gratify the five outer senses. They who look toward the heights, are invulnerable to honor or contempt, praise or dispraise.

"For what you see, that too become you must;

God if you see God - dust if you see dust."

To look upward with the mystic eye is to start on the saving Path of Light. "Look unto Me, and be ye saved (Is 45:22) – I will turn away your captivity from before your eyes – when ye turn unto Me seeking My face." (Jer 29:14)

The farther toward the celestial zenith we send the limitless eye, the deeper is our assurance of our own divine origin and transcendent Selfhood. For truly the Highest is the nearest, the most distant yet most present and we are in His image. The Highest and the Inmost are one.

If then there be any incorporeal eye, let it come forth from the body, to the Vision of the Beautiful. Let it fly up and be lifted into the air; not figure, not body, not ideas, but rather the Maker of these: The Quiet, The Serene, The Stable, The Invariable, The Self, The One - the Like to Itself which neither is like to another.

In high moments of recognition of the Light that transcends reason, we transcend ourselves and write more wisely than we know. No one in his wits attains prophetic truth and inspiration, but when the inspired word is received, the intelligence is enthralled.

Lifting the inner eye to Him who is above reason, lights the two outer eyes to see the world in a new aspect. It gives the tongue new descriptions of the world, and tips the pen with fadeless phrases. And that descending light, compelling transformation of all surrounding objects, is the mystic river of which the angel told Ezekiel. Everything shall live wherever this river flows, and everything on its banks shall be healed.

The healing of the mind to think supernal truth waits upon that light which only the uplifted mystic eye can bring to mind. The transfiguration of matter waits upon the flawless ecstasy, which only the mystic eye can find.

Chapter One – The Silent Edict

Order and beauty hide their sublime mysteries till on the Light's magic Path the tireless vision speeds toward the Origin of beauty and Order.

In heaven there is laid up a pattern which those who choose may behold, and beholding, set their own house in order. The time has now arrived at which they must raise the eye of the soul to the Universal Light, which lightens all things. A reviving miracle of newness falls upon the children of earth when they penetrate beyond the stars to Him who proclaims forever, "Behold, I make all things new." (Rev 21:5)

As balm from the trees of old Gilead in far past days soothed the hurts of the Jews, so the dayspring from on high visits them that sit in darkness and in the shadow of death, to guide their feet into the way of peace.

While we are responsive to the High Edict, lifting up our eye to the smiling Countenance of the Lover ever within us, the Lord of Hosts his name, nothing we can do, or say, or think can quench the down-pouring reconciliation and empowerment or the preserving and healing. He, abiding as the Great Different gives peace, which nothing can invade. His benedictions confer resistless might.

This deathless visional faculty is our only achieving power. It is not dependent upon thoughts of mind or bodily actions, though to them it yields itself day by day in omnipotent servitude.

So eagerly did the untaught seers of the past long to have this immortal faculty find its rightful direction, they willingly practiced mortifications of the body, denied self, affections as well as appetites, to give it freedom. But it asks no such sufferings on the part of the mind or body to give it power to tame and glorify them. It asks only their will that it go homeward.

It is the immaculate of us. Though age and decrepitude have cramped the flesh, senility has sapped the mind, and sickness has blinded the eyes and thickened the ears, yet the wrecked old man lifts up his sightless eyes and smiles. With the immortal and ever young mystical eye, he beholds things celestial. And then he drops the robe of clay, hastening to be identified with his joy-giving vision. Had this eye been lifted to the mountains of help in earlier days, he would have transfigured and renewed his flesh, instead of leaving it to the moth and sod.

With this all-accomplishing sense, we are to repent – to return. "Repent - and turn away your faces from all your abominations which your own powers have made." (Eze 14:6) "Return unto me and I will return unto you." (Mal 3:7). And this is that return which has Divine Reward.

The mind cannot return, "For as the heavens are higher than the earth, so are my thoughts higher than your thoughts." (Is 55:9) The footsteps of flesh cannot return, "For as the heavens are higher than the earth, so are my ways higher than your ways." (Is 55:9) "I have given you an eye divine with which to behold My power." *Upanishads*

By turning the celestial faculty toward the heights we are taken above the thought circuit to the watch: "Watch ye therefore" – "What I say unto you I may say unto all, WATCH." (Mk 13:37) "Blessed are those servants whom the Lord when He comes shall find watching." (Lk 12:37)

All miracle workers have practiced the principle of watching. Moses, the genius for leadership, speaks unto the nation of slaves: "Stand still, and see the salvation of the Lord, which he will show to you." (II Chr 20:17) For the "Lord shall fight for you. And you shall hold your peace." (Ex 14:14)

And this is forever, inevitably, the prayer of the supernally inspired leader of men: "Look down from Thy holy habitation, from heaven, Thy dwelling place, and bless Thy people." (Deut 26:15) And they shall pass in safety through Red Seas of difficulty, though all the powers of mind and matter oppose them.

And this is forever the joyous chant of the liberated people: "He looked to our affliction, and our labor, and our oppression, and He brought us forth out of darkness, with a mighty hand and with an outstretched arm." (Deut 7:7-8) For mystic defense transcends the sharpest swords.

Is it not promised that He will give power unto His two watchers – new powers, miraculous powers! All the forces of the universe cooperate with vision toward beatific ideals. It is not until the eye descends to prowl among the viciousness and crimes of humanity that war and martyrdom succeed.

Elisha never lost his high watch, and even his bones were life giving. His whole pathway on earth was strewn with miracles. For no weapon formed against the comrade of angels can prosper – radiating forever what he assimilates.

Chapter One – The Silent Edict

When the unspoilable region of spiritual health is secretly eyed in diseased patients, they recover. The Hidden Actual readjusts the molecules and atoms of the manifest, to harmonize with the high visional practice.

The world-conquering Jesus crowned the doctrine of the exaltation of the supernal sense with immediate demonstrations: "Father, I will that they may behold my glory." (Jn 17:24) And multitudes came unto Him, and He healed them every one. (Lk 6:19, Matt 12:15)

To the blind man with the clay upon his eyes, He said, "Look up." To all people in times of calamity, He said, "Look up, for your redemption draweth nigh." (Lk 21:28)

This is high mysticism, whether knowingly practiced, as science, or unwittingly and spontaneously exercised, as inspiration. By science, which is the knowledge of invariable orderly processes, inspiration follows speedily. By inspiration, to which great works are easy and masterful deeds are simple, the science comes slowly following after.

The mystics of all ages have trusted their inward eye. While turning it to behold their own personal emotions or affairs they have wrought out no beauty of action or quickening of language. While directing it toward the Un-nameable and Un-describable King of Kings, they have astonished their own age, and all ages, by their miraculous performances and noble aphorisms.

High mysticism calls for highest up-look toward the glory of the Highest.

"Show me, then, O King of all those mystics of superhuman powers, Thy Exhaustless Self. I behold Thee! Thou art of Infinite Valor and Immeasurable Power! Thou art the Primeval God! Thou art the Knower! There is none equal to Thee! O Thou with majesty un-imaged! I behold Thee on all sides!"

By vision toward Transcendence, the meek become awake to Immanence. Omnipresence is but the garment of the Highest. None can find the Tao by discoursing of Omnipresence, Omnipotence or Omniscience. By the uplift of the inner eye toward the countenance of Him who wears these garments, the two outer eyes are baptized with high altar fires to see the glowing land of splendor, through which we ever walk - the finished work.

Chapter One – The Silent Edict

As the mystically opened eyes behold the everywhere-completed splendor the shadows of disorder are not remembered. The soft *alkahest,* universal solvent, dissolves the films of blindness.

Keep your eye on the Eternal and your intellect will grow. There is honor and fortune for those who remember that they are in the presence of the High Cause.

He is by Himself, yet it is to Him that everything owes existence. Becoming eye-witnesses, behold Him, and in beholding, be blessed. He is not light but the Cause that light is. He is not mind, but the Cause that mind is. He is not spirit, but the Cause that spirit is. Let us lay hold of The Beginning, and we shall attain to the contemplation.

Those that shall attain to the contemplation, it detains and attracts as the magnet stone the iron. But now as yet we are not intent upon the vision. So many people are body devotees they can never behold the Vision of the Beautiful. Why, O humanity, have you given yourself over to death, having power to partake of immortality?

Some sages of old spoke of returning to the High Deliverer. Returning to the Root means rest. Those who regulate their attitude by Him will become one with Him. "He is the good person's treasure and the bad person's deliverer."

For those who worship Him, committing to Him all actions, regarding Him as the Supreme End, and turning to nothing else, for them He becomes without delay, the rescuer from the ocean of death-bearing, migratory existence.

By reason of His being the Onlooker the universe revolves. Those devoted to the gods go to the gods; to the ancestors go those devoted to ancestors. Those go to the evil spirits who worship them, and His worshipper also comes to Him. He is beyond the destructible and superior even to the indestructible. Therefore, in the Vedas, He is called The Supreme. Whosoever sees The Supreme sees indeed.

The ancient Hebrews filled their scrolls with the prophecies of the day when humanity should look to the far heights for the opening of their outer eye to see the supernal lands through which they travel daily, stumbling with downcast eyes. And the pages of their sacred books blaze with inspired urgings to greet the onlooking Deity. All eyes shall be toward the Lord. The Lord shall be seen over them, and the

Chapter One – The Silent Edict

Lord of hosts shall defend them. Say unto the cities of Judah, "Behold your God" – "Seek ye Me and ye shall live."

The saving effects of the exalted attention are often times proclaimed by the psalmists: "Because thou hast made the Most High, thy habitation; there shall no evil befall thee, neither shall any plague come nigh thy dwelling." (Ps 91:9) Who is like unto Him who exhalteth Himself to dwell on high? He raises the poor out of the dust that He may set them with princes.

History discloses that no word of self disparagement or thought of fear counts against the saving grace that hastens to defend, or against the tender mercy that upholds, when that deathless soul faculty, the inner eye, lifts toward the Absolute beyond the Light, where not Spirit, but the Cause that Spirit is, does ever call, "Behold who has created."

"We have no might against this great company that cometh against us; neither know we what to do: but our eyes are upon Thee."(II Chr 20:12). The difficulties, inherited difficulties, and causes for discouragement flee away.

Speech follows the direction of the visional sense. Our words therefore soon expose why we are unfortunate or triumphant, great or inconsequent.

Therefore will I direct my prayer unto Thee, whom my outer eyes behold not, and I will look up. Early in the morning I will lift up mine eyes unto Thee.

It is the lifting up of this sense out of the network of materiality, the wheel of incessant grind, which takes us above our disasters and difficulties.

One above looks toward us and toward our affairs. He is of purer eyes than to behold evil. Looking unto Him gives some gleams of His view, for, "In thy light shall we see light." (Ps 36:9) For the angel of the Lord encamps round about them, that have the single-eye that fills the body with light, and delivers them. Thus shall the bodily world become free from old age and death, from corruption and decay, forever and ever.

Ignorance counts nothing against those whose attention is steadfastly set toward the Countenance shining as the sun with healing strength. For they shall all be taught of the High Supreme, not wisdom, but the Cause that wisdom is. "Thus shall I magnify myself, and I will be known in the eyes of many nations." (Ezek 38:23) "And I will show thee great and mighty things, which you know not of." (Jer 33:3)

The Original of Wisdom has abundant store of new information. He gives in liberal measure when He is sought as the Author of intelligence.

Therefore exalt Him and He shall shed light upon you, and upon all the inhabitants of the earth. By repetition the attention of wandering-eyed and weak-minded people is welded toward the saving and illuminating heights.

For by the obedience of one shall many shine forth. Speak unto Him face to face, and no longer speak of Him. Speak unto Him over and over.

No sage of earth has ever declared himself any other than a seeker after the way of the Light that can raise the dead and heal the foolish. But Jesus of Nazareth said, "I am the way; I am the life, I am the truth." (Jn 14:6) "I have overcome the world." (Jn 16.33) The woman at the well said, "I know that Messias cometh, which is called Christ: when he is come, he will tell us all things," (Jn 4:25) and Jesus of Nazareth said, "I that speak unto thee am He." (Jn 4:26)

Martha, the sister of the dead Lazarus said, "I know that my brother shall rise again in the resurrection, at the last day" (Jn 11:24), and Jesus responded, "I am the resurrection." (Jn 11:25)

Jesus demonstrated His declarations by prompt proofs. He set the bands of death at naught, by saying, "No man taketh My life from Me, I lay it down myself." (Jn 10:18) He nullifies the limitations of matter as, looking up, He multiplies food and walks upon the waters. He transcends death exhibiting to all a body, risen in triumphant glory, that cannot be absorbed into death.

He is setting His seal upon the doctrine that all great transactions come into manifestation by reason of the right view of some steadfast seer. "And Jesus looking up, cried with a loud voice, Lazarus come forth," and the dead man arose. (Jn 11:43)

On the three circuits where He found humanity struggling, He met them with the reviving elixirs of the heavenly vision, and caused them to outdo themselves. With right glance and right speech we can superintend the animate and inanimate.

Chapter One – The Silent Edict

On the first circuit, He stretches out His hand and touches wine, bread and clay, and they obey His will to step out of their captivity to habit. The wines of the mystic islands rise through the Cana waters. Bread unfolds from the ether's mysterious opulence. Clay hides the sightless eyeballs till the eye divine sends healing light, and clay shows strange hidden fire as the child of Nain quickens to life.

Jesus finds people appreciating the tangible and material things of life, and He blesses the material things with something from above, but He says, "Flesh profiteth nothing." (Jn 6:23)

On the second circuit, he sends forth His voice and there is overplus of increase for the needy, and His hearers learn the mystery of the Logos, alive in every spoken word baptized by beams from the life-giving God. He finds certain of His hearers advocating the power of thought, urging the dominion of mind, and he blesses the thoughts of mind with something from above. He says: "I will give you a mouth and wisdom," (Matt 6:25,31,34, Matt 10:19) but He also says: "In such an hour as ye think not," (Matt 24:44) and "Take no thought." (Lk 12:11,22 Mk 13:11)

On the third circuit, He warms the fishermen with coals not kindled by human hands, and prepares them to live henceforth by the dispensation of daily miracles wrought from above, that they may be the joy and enlightenment of ages to come.

All the transforming power, which He uses on matter and mind, He draws from above. He teaches plainly that matter and mind must forever keep within restricted bounds of performance, until the whole world looks up and draws down authority to unseal their limitations. "Canst thou by taking thought *alone* make one hair white or black?" (Matt 5:36) "Blessed are those servants whom the Lord when he cometh shall find watching." (Lk 12:37)

Those who set their attention toward the Countenance of the High and Lofty One inhabiting Eternity, are in the way of the ransomed from sin, disorder and death. And the ransomed are offered two songs: "The Song of Moses, and the Song of the Lamb." (Rev 15:3)

A song is a perpetually recurring note of speech or singing, concerning some one theme. The ransomed return with singing. They know the Name of the Highest, which stands among humanity for The Absolute as Origin of Being, Might, Majesty. This Name was the song of Moses, personification of strength in leadership by the inspiration of Deity.

Chapter One – The Silent Edict

It is the Name taken up by all who lift the incorporeal eye toward the Author of Being, Might and Majesty. It is as immaculate as the vision that is uplifted. It is not the final name of the Cause of Being, Cause of Truth, Cause of Spirit; for a proper name for the Father, the Un-begotten, is not yet known among humankind. These terms, Father, God, Creator, Lord are not names, but terms of address derived from His benefits and works.

But the Name, which is called the Song of Moses, is the highest name that can be spoken by us at our present stage of expression. It has no reference to benefits or works. It stands by itself alone. It is applied to no other but One. It is, *I Am That I Am.* The term of address, or name God, stands for many objects of worship; the substantive Spirit, has many significations, it may mean one of twenty different descriptives; the name in ten different ways, but the *I Am That I Am* is One. "When the children of Israel shall say: "What is His name? What shall they answer?" "Say the *I Am* hath sent thee."

And He led them with His glorious arm, dividing the waters before them, to make for Himself an everlasting Name.

The Name *I Am*, addressed to the Highest, wakens the spirit of authority, majesty, undefeatable courage, in the breast of even the meekest and weakest of us. "I have wrought with you for My Name's sake."

The Name, *I Am That I Am,* brings up from the deep wells of hidden strength in all people the sincerity, boldness and intelligence of leadership, and that originality of action and language which have characterized the heroes of the ages whose names have lived so long in history that they have become myths.

It is recorded that Moses, in deepest humility, asking of the Self-Existent face to face, His most order-bringing Name, heard the words, *Ahmi Yot Ahmi – I Am That I Am,* and this man became ruler of a kingdom, and founder of the Wisdom of the Magi. He had touched the leading note of that Ineffable Name which is key to the mysteries of the universe.

This Name is the first utterance of those who set their attention toward the Heights, from where fall the kindling sparks that burn away the films hiding the finished splendor of the realm through which we walk.

Chapter One – The Silent Edict

And the Song of the Lamb is the second utterance of the upward-visioned among us. It is the name *Jesus Christ*. "In my Name," said He that was slain. "In His Name," said His disciples. And it is declared that they never preached any doctrine except the power of His Name. This was their Song. It is a Name as immaculate as the Name *I Am*. It always means, God with us – Emmanuel. It is that Name of the Lofty and Everlasting *I Am* which represents His nearness and immanence. The Name *Jesus Christ* is above principalities and powers. It is the Name of newness, of healing, and of comforting tenderness. It gives the baptism of the quickening Spirit. It is the greatest and quickest God-formulating Name. It is the Name that restores the lost word, the now unspeakable Name of the Self-Existent Deity.

The Moravians hymn the power of this Name: "Should I reach my dying hour only let them speak that name. By its all prevailing power, back my voice returns again." And they tell of miracles of calling back from the dark defile of voiceless death to sunlit life, by the resurrecting energy of His Name. The rulers of the Jews in Jerusalem knew well the magian power contained in certain names, and they asked, "By what name have you wrought this miracle?" "By the Name of Jesus Christ," answered the Christian Apostles.

The risen Christ, appearing suddenly, said, "Preach repentance… in My Name…. Beginning at Jerusalem" (Lk 24:47) And Jerusalem means The Self.

Begin with yourself to repent, to return. Lift up the willing inner sight toward the Supreme One, whose Soundless Edict through the ages is, "Look unto Me, and be ye saved." (Is 45:22) Taste the first manna, which the upward watch sprinkles over the unfed brain and heart.

Facing toward the Heights, where the smile of the Comforting One begins its beaming Omnipresence, Omnipotence, and Omniscience, speak from the heart the two greatest Names ever written or spoken on earth. They are the only response the heart can make when the mystic eye is first uplifted.

Without the uplift of the deathless sense, the Names may be but heathen repetitions. For liberation is not achieved by the pronunciation of the Name without direct perception. But consonant with the upward watch, these terms of address to Deity are the planting of the feet upon the rock of power and the hills of security.

"He sent from above, He took me, He drew me out of many waters. Thou also hast lifted me up on high, above them that rose up against me."

Chapter One – The Silent Edict

Whatever comes upon you this day, or threatens to disturb, or over-throw you at any time, turn then from it toward that High Deliverer and within the silent heart, sing the two Wonderful Songs of the Seers of the ages:

O High and Lofty One inhabiting Eternity! Clothing Thyself with Thine own Omnipresence, Omnipotence and Omniscience, as with a garment - hiding Thy goodness and majesty with names, and unspeakable names! I know Thou Art, and the Name of power and glory I must address to Thee is, "I Am."

O Countenance beholding me! Looking toward me through the ages! Breath of the everlasting life in me, and manna to my fadeless substance - Thy Name that folds me round with tenderness, and lifts me high above the pitfalls of my human destiny, is "Jesus Christ."

Practice

Bible verses to commit to memory.

- "The Lord looketh upon all the inhabitants of the earth."(Ps 33:14)

- "Look unto me and be ye saved, all the ends of the earth; for I am God and there is none else." (Is 45:22)

- "What I say unto you, I say unto all, Watch!" (Mk 13:37)

- "I will guide thee with mine eye." (Ps 32:8)

- "Great, the Mighty God, great in counsel and mighty in work." (Jer 32:19)

- "I will instruct thee and teach thee." (Ps 32:8)

- "Repent, and turn away your faces, from all your abominations."(Eze 4:6)

- "Behold, he cometh with clouds; and every eye shall see him." (Rev 1:7)

- "They sing the song of Moses, and the song of the Lamb." (Rev 15:3)

- "That led them by the right hand of Moses with his glorious arm, dividing the waters before them, to make himself an everlasting name." (Is 63:12)

> "He raiseth the poor up out of the dust that He may set him with princes." (Ps 113:7-8)

> "That repentance should be preached in his name, beginning at Jerusalem." (Lk 24:17)

> "There is none other name under heaven given among men, whereby we must be saved." (Acts 4:12)

Résumé - Monday First Week

The High and Lofty One inhabiting Eternity has been understood by His lovers to be forever inviting humanity to look unto His Countenance shining as the Sun with healing strength.

The Deity looks upon us; let us look to the Deity. This is the way of salvation from sin, sickness, misfortune, and death.

Isaiah understood it as a Soundless Mandate: "Look unto me and be ye saved, all the ends of the earth." (Is 45:22) Ezekiel understood it as the law of repentance, or returning: "Repent, and turn away your faces from all your abominations." (Eze 14:6) Jesus called it the Watch: "What I say unto you, I say unto all, Watch" (Mark 13:37).

It has been found that what we vision steadily causes our thinking. We secretly perceive toward an object before thinking it.

What we call our "me" is that to which we most often set our visional sense. It can be set either toward God or toward the workings of our own brain.

We will choose the "Great, the Mighty God, great in counsel and mighty in work" (Jer 32:19), for our objective. This is the way of being God-taught. "I will instruct thee and teach thee" (Ps 32:8). It is the way of being divinely guided. "I will guide thee with mine eye." (Ps 32:8)

John the Revelator was God-taught. He saw all truth in symbols, or pictures. He called the great lessons he learned, *Angels, or Messages*. He divided them into seven. The seventh he repeats over and over, like Joshua sounding one tone with rams' horns on the seventh day of his circling of Jericho. The tone John sounds is, *"I looked,"* and, *"I beheld"*.

Chapter One – The Silent Edict

"With obedience to the mandate, "Look unto me," (Is 45:22) John saw hail and fire mingled with blood, fall upon the earth (Rev. 8).

Hail is new fresh truth. How can we help having new truth if we set our eye in a new direction? It is the resistless truth of the eternal Heights.

Fire is the emblem of heavenly fervor. The heart flames up with new zeal, new ardor, and new love, if the vision is upward.

Blood is the emblem of new life. There are those who can appear who were not born of the will of humankind but of the will of God. They sometimes appear in our own age. Two were seen by a highway robber to be walking along with a missionary at midnight when the missionary supposed himself to be alone. The robber hurried away from the three of them.

This is the new life we cannot help encountering as we seek our highest Good at the highest Source. The disciples felt their hearts burn while they talked with the one who appeared to them as they walked toward Emmaus. Their frequent gaze had been heavenward where, on the right hand of God Omnipotent, they had envisioned their Lord and Master, Jesus the Christ.

Because of their upward watch, the empowering Angel of God's Presence was tangible to them. Such appearances are the blood of obedience.

John the Revelator sees a third of the trees disappear. He sees all the green grass burn up (Rev. 8). *Trees* are the emblems of flourishing practices. One-third of these practices cease, in the life of the individual, as the flaming zeal for God kindles. Competitive examinations, competitive trades, and competitive platforms, which constitute the ginger and glow of the non-visioning life, cease. For they know that their true provisions and their true positions come straight from above, and nothing and nobody can take them from them.

Everything that is strenuous in any way must cease. The laborers and anarchists, the pole hunters and the gold grabbers must calm down. The Countenance that shines hot with healing tenderness and with rich giving is of more value than all that can possibly come by the clash of endeavor.

Grass is emblem of the seasons of human life, childhood, youth, middle age, and old age, such as the new people know not.

Chapter One – The Silent Edict

The visional sense that seeks the Vast Countenance ever shining toward us, can bring back news of any objective it sets itself toward, from the rocks of the gorges to the midnight stars.

Obeying the sublime mandate, "Look unto me," (Is 45:22) we sense the mystery of redemptive energy. John tells us that the Redeemed are given two songs (Rev. 15). The name, *I Am That I Am,* was the song of Moses and the name *Jesus Christ*, was the song of the first Christians. These names are full of the meaning of life and the transports of Eternal Truth.

I Am That I Am is the name of kingly might and majesty. Some who repeated the name often stepped out of the rank and file of men into the rulership of the nations.

"The Lord is high above all nations and his glory above the heavens. Who is like unto the Lord our God who exalteth himself to dwell on high? He raiseth the poor up out of the dust that He may set him with princes (Ps. 113:4-8)

With that Name, which means that no one knows the nature and character of Him that bears it, Moses led two million slaves to triumphant liberty: "That led them by the right hand of Moses with his glorious arm, dividing the waters before them, to make himself an everlasting name. (IS 63)

With the Song of the Lamb in his heart, Peter converted three thousand people to Christianity by one transcendent sermon. "There is none other name under heaven given among men, whereby we must be saved," he said (Acts 4:12).

Let us take Monday to repent, to turn away our faces from all the things, events and people that call our attention. Let us often look upward toward the Deity ever beholding us. Let us tell that *Ain Soph*, Great Countenance of the Absolute above thinking and above being, as the Kabbalah avers, that we know His Name of uplifting might; His Name of majesty and grandeur. It is *I Am That I Am*.. Let us tell Him that we know His Name of manifestation in the flesh, His embodying Name, His Name of our own manifested health and undefeatable free Spirit. This Name is *Jesus Christ*.

It is on the principle of doing things in order, as Paul enjoined, (I Cor. 14:40) that we begin the week days with obedience to the heavenly ordinance, "Look unto Me," which is preaching repentance beginning at Jerusalem, or the Self (Luke 24:47)

Chapter Two – Remission, Denial of all but God

Tuesday, First Week

2nd Gate - **There is no mixture of evil in my good. There is no opposition to my God as material conditions of any kind. There is no absence of life, substance, or intelligence. There is nothing to hate. There is no presence of sin, sickness, or death in my world, where God is the only presence and power and wisdom.**

We are so constituted that when we are told that the Divine Edict is, "Look unto Me," (Is 45:22) we lift our inner visional sense to look toward the High Cause, the Vast, Vast Countenance that shines as the sun. The beams of that Countenance are hot with healing.

Something is ever gently wooing us. It is the sin-undoing Saving Grace. It rides swiftly to our freedom on the thrill of our recognition. Every beam of light and every waft of air from sighting toward the Unsullied Heights, is the touch of the dissolving *Alkahest*, the remitting mystery, the saving grace, removing some suffering, exposing some joy. Is it not written, "Look unto Me, and be ye saved?" (Is 45:22)

Jesus, the One who has been utterly set free from the might of the flesh and its death, rose, as untrammeled Being, and said, "Preach Remission." (Lk 24:27) Preach the removal, the putting away of the consequences of the downward vision, which appear as evil, matter, lack, pain, and decay. Preach the freedom of those who notice that Deity on-looks them.

A principle is a comprehensive law. They who look to the Unweighted First Cause are unweighted of sickness. "Behold, I will lay thy foundation with sapphires or liberty."(Rev. 21:19) "They shall fight against thee; but they shall not prevail against thee."(Jer 1:19)

The mind is not capable of bringing anything to pass except it be transfixed by inward visioning. Inner vision is the vital essential to the mind. When this faculty is exalted, the mind quickens with original ideas and has high instructions. We secretly perceive toward an object before thinking it, and it is only by having constant recourse by inward viewing that the mind goes on to know and comprehend.

The High and Lofty One inhabiting Eternity, offers to undo our weakness and our wretchedness even the laws of matter and the veneers of time, if we seek only His face. He offers a new language and the end of the world: "Look up to the fields white for the harvest."(Jn 4:35) "The harvest is the end of the world."(Matt 13:39) "They shall speak with new tongues."(Mk 16:17)

We are like those we face, dropping their unlikeness. It is not strange, then, to find the mystics of all times joyously exclaiming that the Undifferentiated Self-Existent, the Abysmal Naught, has remitted for them the five dark unlikenesses to Himself into which their aberrated watch had warped them. They have not been seeking liberation from bondage, they have only been seeking His face, according to the Sacred Edict, "Look unto Me."(Is 45:22) Yet liberation has been as complete through the ecstatic moments of their contemplation as if they had entered Paradise.

The experiences of the mystics have been reported as the shouts of the free. Their shouts have been the creedal formulas of philosophic and religious organizations without number. The zealous lovers of the formulas have often forgotten that matter does not loose the grip of its law if the vision is not toward the heights.

Evil lets go its claims only when the Dayspring from on high drops its dewy sunshine into the heart. "I will turn back your captivity before your eyes, said the Lord."(Jer 29:14)

High mysticism is divine nihilism. Truly, there is no knowledge except what is taught straight from Him who said, "I will instruct thee, and teach thee."(Ps 32:8) Truly, there is safety from drowning for whoever looks away from the stormy waters of human existence to Him who said, "The flames shall not kindle, the waters shall not overflow." (Is 43:2) "Nothing shall by any means hurt you."(Lk 10:19)

It is preaching remission when we tell the Unweighted Light face to face, that we know our surety of unburdened life under His healing smile. It is a prayer; and prayer is ever a psalm of freedom.

If the vision be on high - where the illimitable skies in untrammeled buoyancy shine chastely down - purity of moral tone and flawlessness of body are manifest. Vanity, deception, and cowardice are remitted and dissolved. Sickness, weakness, and disease are removed. The original Self, denuded of its density, forgets its history in matter. The former earth is forgotten. It does not come into mind any more.

Chapter Two – Remission, Denial of all but God

He unto whose face we look has vouchsafed to no one His Name, and none as yet knows His nature. We know His promises, His gifts, His responses; but we have nothing more sublime than Life, Love, and Spirit, of which He is the Giver, to describe. It is because our inward visional sense has been engaged in fetching either gladness or sorrow from other objectives than from His glory.

Life, Love, and Spirit are His gifts and belong already among our tangible and practical experiences. It is not surprising that the subtler triumphs undergirding those who have sought the Giver, and not the gifts, have not been understood. For only the Original of knowing can say, "I will show thee great and mighty things which thou knowest not." (Jer 3:33)

Life and Love may not say, "Look unto me and be ye masters of life." They may not go higher than repletion with their like. Only their Author is their Master, and only he can confer mastership. "All the nations shall fear and tremble for all the goodness and for all the prosperity that I procure thee, saith the Lord." Thou canst not behold me with thy two outer eyes; I have given thee an eye divine."

Concerning the Almighty, we cannot find Him out…with God is terrible majesty. "Behold God is great, and we know him not."(Job 36:26)

Paul declared the Unknown God who gives life and spirit. He could not describe His nature. He did not know any Name for God greater than *I Am That I Am*. But it was immortalizing to Paul himself to call the gaze higher than life and spirit to the *Ain Soph* of the Kabbalah, - the Great Countenance of the Absolute, above thinking and above being.

"My Father is greater than I,"(Jn 14:28) was the upward calling statement of Jesus; and because His eye was ever toward the Divine Original, He was ever Master of life. "I can lay down my life…and I can take up my life, he said. (Jn 10:18)

We need not fear to let go of all that dissolves under the high watch. No one can see that Face and live according to his former estate. The former estate shall shuffle off – be remitted.

Sell all, let all move aside – let go, and give to the One Poor, The Unknowable Absolute, The Unhindered God, The Unweighted *I Am*, the Predicateless Being. This is the universal insistence of inspired mystics. We have only one thing to give, namely, our attention. There is only One Poor, namely The Unencumbered First

Chapter Two – Remission, Denial of all but God

Cause. "Who holdeth fast to The High First Cause, of him the world shall come in quest."

Preach the deliverance of the captive. Acknowledge high. Tell the One High Cause, that being Untrammeled Freedom in himself, all who look to him are untrammeled. Tell him that fear and doubt depart. Tell him that captivity itself is led captive, and only unvanquished Soul salutes him.

The dissolving *alkahest*, the gentle grace that falls down over the track of the high vision, has been praised by the sages of the ages, for there is surcease of world pain in its white softness. Behold the gentle Neutral that takes away the mistakes of the world!

Five grievous shades slip off the earth. They are the foolish virgins with no oil of healing and no oil of illuminating in their most eloquent declarations. No one describing them was ever to himself or to his neighbor the oil of joy for mourning, or the inspiration of wisdom while detailing the processes. It is the passing of these five shadows that has caused the five great shouts of liberty, the psalms of remission, the prayers of the released:

- Steadfastly facing Thee, there is no evil on my pathway.
- Steadfastly facing Thee, there is no matter with its laws.
- Steadfastly facing Thee, there is no loss, no lack, no absence, and no deprivation.
- Steadfastly facing Thee, there is nothing to fear, for there shall be no power to hurt.
- Steadfastly facing Thee, there is neither sin, nor sickness, nor death.

Preach remission, said the Risen Christ. Preach that the stone of interference looming on our life path is rolled away. Preach that palsy falls off, death falls off. O thou Unshaken One - by thy favor my delusions are destroyed!

Matter with its laws of mind are the fictitious generations of much downward glancing with our efficient visional sense. When this sense is lifted up, what seemed external exists no more at all. The inner vision leads off the other senses and, if exalted toward the Healing Onlooker, all the senses aver health. "For I am the Lord that healeth thee." (Ex 15:26) "The way of life is above to the wise that he may depart from hell beneath." (Prov 15:24) "Seek ye my face and live." (Amos 5:6)

Chapter Two – Remission, Denial of all but God

A very subtle doctrine explains, that we are like that to which our inner eye is most often directed. It has been called the secret doctrine, because whoever discourses on the laws of mind, or describes the Omnipresence of Life, Truth and Spirit, has not touched the secret of Deity's look toward them and their look toward Deity. The secret doctrine is denuding even of Spirit. "Blessed are the poor in Spirit." (Matt 5:3) Something transcending Spirit smiles. Let the spirit blow where it listeth. "There is no one who has power over the Spirit. For Spirit is the servant of the High Deliverer – the I Am That I Am. "Behold, I will pour out my Spirit upon you." (Prov 1:23)

The Deity who looks toward us, saying, "Look unto Me," (Is 45:22) is not Spirit, for Spirit arises in opposition to matter, and the Deity is above distinction. Only those who perceive the Lord as Difference-less, go to the Supreme End.

God is not Being, for there is an arising of contradistinction. He cannot be called goodness, for goodness is opposed to badness. God is above this distinction.

Deity is best described by negations, since only His gifts are knowable. He is not that! We may insist to all descriptions of Deity.

Specialists multiply that which they investigate. There shall never be an understanding of how fadeless health is roused, so long as the physical system that faithful register of woe and vigor brought on the wings of secret viewing is sought as the informer. Only by the study of the Uncontaminated One, who inhabits Eternity shall unspoilable wholesomeness laugh in the substance of all living creatures. Only His way upon the earth is the saving health of the nations.

The material body is a hard taskmaster. What it ought to be fed with and how it should be housed and trained – see how it worries us with never telling us. The sons of the Tao know that neither if they eat are they the better, nor if they eat not are they the worse. Every mouthful shines with new mystery, and buoys up the system as on wings of might; every abstinence leaves the veins free for the sunshine of the Beautific Uplands to flow along in radiant strength. Who can prove this till he has often time torn his gaze from the wheel of things to behold the Unencumbered Highest?

The mind is a wearisome objective. Its thoughts have laid claim to great powers of destruction and great powers of building. With the brightness of the I Am beaming upon them, even their wrath is praise of the Unthinkable Absolute. Jesus can look

Chapter Two – Remission, Denial of all but God

around with anger, being grieved and the withered arm stretches forth, restored whole as the other.

Under the baptism of the Divine Smile, the wickedness of the wicked shall not destroy, and the righteousness of the righteous shall not save. The Tender Mercy, the Dayspring from on high, remits the thoughts of the mind.

Our inheritance of things that have not been conceived by mind comes into sight by looking to the Unknowable, who originates new knowing. "I will teach thee." "I will turn to the people a pure language."

Those who watch for the erroneous thought that caused the malady of a neighbor shall find it alighting upon themselves. The watchers for iniquity shall be cut off.

All the ways of darkness are removed by the Light that falls with remitting grace upon those who notice that the Deity looks upon them. "Look up to the fields white for the harvest." The harvest is the end of the world. "Speak ye comfortably to Jerusalem. Tell her that her warfare is accomplished."

There is only one Universal Solvent. It is the falling *alkahest*. The whiteness that makes death let go - that looses the bands of palsy and of pain. There is no pain, facing Thee.

Steadfastly looking for high news, we find that evil has no substance, that matter is nothing. Hezekiah rises in free majesty because "The earth and all the inhabitants thereof are dissolved." Isaiah finds that "All nations before Him are as nothing, and they are counted unto him as less than nothing." Job, meekest of all under the ever-beholding Solvent, yields himself in joyous dissolution – "Thine eyes are upon me, and I am not."

The assurances of the mystics have ever been that all the hurting powers are nullified - remitted, for those who look away to the Divine Original.

"No weapon formed against thee shall prosper."(Is 54:17)

"No bad fame can hurt thee."(Lk 10:19)

"Thou shalt be far from oppression."(Is 54:14)

Chapter Two – Remission, Denial of all but God

"Terror shall not come near thee."(Ps 91: 7, 10)

The accepted formula of the mystics has not been that the world is divine, and all things are God, but the world is no-thing – the Lofty One inhabiting Eternity is The Alone – The All.

Looking downward, we weep at loss and lack, while the offer has ever been that there shall be no lack for the beholders of the smile of the *Ain Soph*. They shall want for no good thing facing Thee.

Our stress and strain on every line desist - we no longer labor, we take no thought. Looking to the Heights, away from labor and lack, the way is visible. "I will lead thee by the way thou hast not known." (Is 42:16) "The people shall not say I am sick."(Is 33:24) "They shall not see death."(Ps 89:48) "I am the Lord that healeth thee."(Ex 15:26)The truth is that matter and mind no longer hinder us, as the beams of the Shining Countenance penetrate to the hidden heart. The mystical vision and union gives us that most divine knowledge of Almighty God, which is known through not knowing.

It constitutes that union which enkindles our life flame, giving rest to the soul now fled up, away from evil, to the place free from evils. How worthwhile to view above time and sense, preaching the inevitable remission, taking the instructions of the sages of the ages who have experienced it.

Sometimes these great forerunners have called our mental, moral, and physical characteristics and comports, our garments folded around in our descent to view the not-God. And they show how one by one these garments have fallen from them on their upward-fleeing vision. Love of honor is the last garment to be stripped away, as we show ourselves more like the Divine.

According to all these illumined ones, it is the Omnipotence through all things that binds them all in such sympathy. The crawling worm is brother to the archangel, in the fact of his central spark being God. Wherever remission is experienced, there is the miracle of the creature divinely transcending environment. Preaching remission uncovers the divinity at the center, because it entices the eye heavenward whence the uncovering day-springs hail.

Chapter Two – Remission, Denial of all but God

The illuminati of the world have been at all times living proofs of the efficiency of setting the watch toward the Self-Existent Heights. Each one manifested according to their very own recognition of the Supreme.

Unto some, it is the manifest readjustment of environment. Unto others, it is the forgetfulness of environments. Unto some, it is joy in shining health of body. Unto others, it is the forgetfulness that the body exists.

Union with divine Freedom, the heavenly Poor, is fraught with resultants near and far. The world receives a treatment as the pioneer on high plains unifies with the free light. The watcher shines forth as the sun with the healing glory of the Father above. The world awaits the great Peace Treatment.

Whether the Unweighted Heights are sought in coldly scientific mood or in religious warmth to inspire the particular from the Universal - that which would hedge the free self removes. "Watch the Way," said Nahum, "so fortifying thy powers mightily."

Ezra is scientific: "I will lift up mine eyes to the hills, from whence cometh my help," (Ps 121:1) but he makes haste to be religious: "I have gone astray like a lost sheep; seek thy servant, Lord. "Great peace have they which love thy law and nothing shall offend them."(Ps 119:165)

Learning to gaze upward toward the Father's Face is a liberating act. It rouses fresh hope. It puts us on the pathway of salvation from the causes of calamity.

Our Free, Wise, Immortal Center is the begotten of God. Only this Shining Principle is Offspring of *I Am That I Am*. It cannot be injured. Not only the free and unspoilable soul, spirit, of Jesus, but the soul, the hidden spark of Nero, is Son of the Highest. Jesus being unclothed of matter with its mind and temper; Nero being heavily garmented therewith. The upward vision saves Nero or Jesus. The upward vision saves all. There is no respect of persons on the High Watch. "Mine eyes are ever toward the Lord; for he shall pluck my feet out of the net" maybe proclaimed by good or bad alike.

The remission loved by those who lift their eyes to the Predicateless One in this age, is the removal of the hurting powers of life and death, riches and poverty, sin and virtue. They look for the day of Wisdom to break, and the shadowy night of ignorance to flee away.

Chapter Two – Remission, Denial of all but God

The ordinance of the Highest, "Look unto Me" (Is 45:22) requires an individual practice. It compels a life of its own. It exposes the doctrine known to Jesus of Nazareth, who said, "If any man will do His will, he shall know of the doctrine."(Jn 7:17)

At the point of knowing right doctrine, an influence emanates which clarifies all atmospheres. The neighbors of the knower drop their errors of thought and conduct. They start to seek the highest good at the highest fountain.

As we are gazing toward the One and Indivisible, the phenomenal world with its origination and decrease, multiplicity and diversity is non-existent and illusion.

The watcher loves and preaches the High Eternal I Am, whose assurance is union by vision. The heart would praise and extol Him whose look toward us remits all unlike His own nature. To the real heart there is joy in the divine fact that there are treasures of knowledge laid up for those whose true foundation is freedom by the look of their God upon them.

Mental and bodily hindrances are dissolved and set aside. To the heart, there is gladness in knowing that remitted conditions leave exposed the Secret Original Self from which transcendent character springs forth, daily honoring the Father with the beauty of Soul Integrity.

The second angel sounds and we acknowledge the liberty which comes from obeying the high mandate. The mountain of all personal obligations rolls into the sea. The *I Am That I Am* of Unspeakable Majesty is seen to be the only Responsible One. Only Untrammeled God is real. "Is there a God beside me? - I know not any."(Is 44:8) Anxiety is no more.

Obedient watchers heavenward walk the buoyant path of fearlessness. They burst the bonds of desire and its attainment. They breathe above ambition. The wonderful God makes them preachers of the heavenly remission. They tell of Him who is above Truth, whose very works are truth. They tell of Him who saves from old age, death, disease, poverty, ignorance, and competition.

"Destroyed is the knot in the heart, removed are all doubts; Extinct are all the hidden longings upon beholding Thee." Let us set aside a day to telling over to Him unto whose Divine Countenance we look, the wonderful remissions, the heavenly liberations promised to those who oft-time turn away from smothering environments, to face the Lover inhabiting Eternity – the Lord of Hosts His name. Let us boldly acknowledge, as we lift up our eyes unto the Deliverer, the Limitless: *"Because Thou art The Unconditioned and The Absolute, I also am unconditioned and absolute. Because Thou art The Free, I also am free. Because Thou art The Self-Existent, I also am self-existent."*

Practice

Bible verses to commit to memory.

- "That remission should be preached in all nations beginning at Jerusalem."(Lk 24:47)

- "Then Peter said unto them, Repent, and be baptized every one of you in the name of Jesus Christ for the remission of sins, and ye shall receive the gift of the Holy Ghost."(Acts 2:38)

- "Look diligently lest any man fail of the grace of God."(Heb 12:15)

- "Facing Thee, there is nothing to fear, for nothing shall by any means hurt me."(Lk 10:19)

- "Thou dissolvest my substance."(Job 30:22)

- "The earth and all the inhabitants thereof are dissolved."(Ps 75:3)

- "If any man will come after me, let him deny himself."(Matt 16:24)

- "When men are cast down thou shalt say, There is lifting up, and God shall save the humble person."(Job 22:29)

- "They shall want for no good thing."(Ps 34:10)

Résumé - Tuesday First Week

It is a principle that what we most often view with the inner eye, will show forth outwardly. This is how we can easily understand why the poor cripple near the temple gate (Acts 3), with vision in the dust, had never felt the dissolving of the manacles of impotence, until Peter and John bade him look up. Something then fell

Chapter Two – Remission, Denial of all but God

down over his upward visioning and undid his chains of mind and body. "Preach remission," (Lk 24:47) said Jesus. Preach the dissolving Grace.

"When men are cast down thou shalt say, there is lifting up, and God shall save the humble person."(Job 22:29) There are shouts of freedom, handed down from antiquity, that represent the experiences of remission, or liberation of the upward watchers throughout the ages. They declare the disappearance of foolishness and ignorance. They recognize that foolish virgins or objectives, with no oil of healing and no oil of illuminating in their sayings, are shut out.

There is no oil of healing and no oil of illuminating in descriptions of evil. Description of evil is a foolish virgin. The description of evil doubles evil. It does not lessen it. See then how foolish it is to describe evil and thereby double it.

If we see an army of locusts alighting on some green vegetation, we mourn because the people must starve. This is our foolishness. We increase starvation by such mourning. According to Jesus, the risen and triumphant man of God, we are to look up to the shining Face of our Father looking tenderly down upon us, and declare, "Steadfastly facing Thee, there is no evil on my pathway." For only abundance and gentle kindness, fall from the Vast Countenance ever shining toward us.

God sees no evil. We catch the viewpoint of those with whom we associate. Let us catch the High God's viewpoint, and go free from sight of evil. "Sing aloud, O daughter of Zion; shout, O Israel! Rejoice and exult with all your heart, O daughter of Jerusalem! The Lord has taken away the judgments against you. He has cast out your enemies. The King of Israel, the Lord, is in your midst; you shall fear evil no more."(Zeph 3:14-15)

Matter also has been found to have no health in its operations. No descriptions of matter quicken the pulses with healing blood, or fill the stomach with strengthening energy. No study of matter illuminates the spiritual wisdom that waits like unlit candles just above our heads. Only the kindling fires of God's hot glance can illuminate our waiting intelligence. We must recognize the glance, acting under obedience to the order "Behold Me."(Is 65:1) Matter moves aside for indestructible free grace to act, when by upward viewing we shout, "Facing Thee, There is no matter with its laws."

Neither is there any oil of healing in descriptions of lack and deprivation. "They shall want for no good thing." (Ps. 34:10) We must preach to the heavens that: "Facing the Father there is neither lack nor deprivation."

Chapter Two – Remission, Denial of all but God

There is no acting free grace visible to one who describes hurts and pains. Peter sank into the raging waters when he took his gaze off the powerful Jesus. (Matt 14) But with his eye uplifted, he walked above the waves, side by side with Omnipotence. There is a shout of liberty any one can give when hurts come grinding and burning upon him: "Facing Thee, There is nothing to fear, for nothing shall by any means hurt me."(Luke 10:19) All hurting power is darkness. The dayspring from on high gives light to them that sit in darkness, to guide their feet into the way of peace. (Luke 1:79)

Sinfulness with its sickness and death is only the description of that which is encountered by those with aberrated vision, or downward gaze. It is gazing downward to describe a child's bad temper or a friend's unkindness. It does not only affect them, but also those who engage into the descriptions.

The shout of the free must be given before we feel freedom. Did not Jesus shout, "It is finished," (Jn 19:30) before it was finished? See how quickly the anguish left him when he shouted with a loud voice, "It is finished." (John 19:30) Let us take Tuesday to shout liberty – free grace – remission – unburdening, as we look upward. Free grace comes softly stealing over the Tao, or Track, of the upward watch. Take the shouts in order. Look up to the Vast Countenance with its beaming and kindling free grace, its dissolving a*lkahest*, ever streaming toward us, and with joyous heart let us proclaim:

Steadfastly facing Thee, there is no evil on my pathway.

Steadfastly facing Thee, there is no matter with its laws.

Steadfastly facing Thee, there is no loss, no lack, no absence and no deprivation.

Steadfastly facing Thee, there is nothing to fear, for there shall be no power to hurt.

Steadfastly facing Thee, there is neither sin, nor sickness, nor death.

Because Thou art The Unconditioned and The Absolute, I also am unconditioned and absolute.

Because Thou art The Omnipotent Free Spirit, I also am omnipotent free spirit.

Because Thou art The Self-Existent, I also am self-existent.

Chapter Three – Forgiveness, Affirmation of all as God

Wednesday, First Week

3rd Gate - **God is all. God is the Omnipresent, Omnipotent, Omniscient Good, as Life, Truth, Love, Substance, and Intelligence. I am my own idea of God. I live, and move and have my being according to my idea of God. I am spirit, mind, like my God, and shed abroad wisdom, strength, and holiness. My God works through me to will and to do that which ought to be done by me. I am governed by the True God. I am kept from sin, from suffering for sin, and I cannot fear sin, sickness, or death.**

This third study is prepared so that even those who have not heard its subject matter orally can understand that the High Vision which awakens high thinking and incites to noble living has been the Vital Theme of the preceding chapters. Something always antedates thought, that something is Vision: "Look unto Me" is the Sacred Edict.

Throughout all time there has been tacit understanding that when half gods go the gods arrive. Some let go of their half gods with tears and lamenting, bemoaning the departure of all earthly helpers. Some take hold of unseen help with groanings and with grim determinations, whereby they painfully earn their blessings, heroically forgetting "Cast all your care…"(I Pet 5:7) "My yoke is easy and my burden is light." (Matt 11:30)

It is the wisdom of Jesus that He urges us to be wide-awake and to let go easily and to catch on to the sprinkling *Alkahests* (*Universal Solvent*) soundless *nepenthe* (*which quells all sorrows with forgetfulness*), ever falling on all our heads. "Hurt not the oil of letting go; nor the wine of healing inspiration."(Rev 6:6) Repent, for remission, receiving the Holy Spirit that alone makes whole.

John the Revelator is not choosing haphazard the chalcedony stone as symbol of the third lesson of divine law. The chalcedony signifies awakening strength: "Awake, awake, put on thy strength, O Zion."(Is 52:1) "Look up to fields white for harvest"(Jn 4:35) so shall old conditions dissolve; so shall the Holy Spirit arrive – white breath that makes strengthening wholeness.

Humankind sticks to a triune of some kind. It is a mysterious instinct. Some call *Three* the number of Divine Law others regard it as a specially complete and mystic number. We may note that this Lesson Three with its wide application holds all the twelve lessons in its norm or pattern, if we read its purport aright.

Whatever way people regarded God, so He manifested Himself to them. The great prophets saw God the Father Almighty, miracle-working Jehovah Triumphant. Apostolic Christians saw God the Son Almighty, miracle-working Jehovah Triumphant. To the Apostles of the Mystical Dispensation God appeared as the Holy Spirit Almighty, miracle-working Jehovah Triumphant, just winging its white influence across our awakening planet.

So far, this third dispensation of the Triune God in the Universe has not shown forth the mighty miracles of the first or prophetic dispensation nor did the second Apostolic dispensation show itself equal in grandeur or performance to the first; but the halt in splendor or achievement has had more universal promise in all that has been done, as if a whole globe were being bathed in softly stealing Brahmic Breath where astonishing whirlwinds had once glued the world's awe-struck attention.

When Moses, legislator of the Hebrew nation and founder of the Jewish religion, called to God, the Father Almighty, to divide the Red Sea, before the Israelites fleeing from Egyptian bondage, he heard his God saying, "Wherefore criest thou unto Me? Speak unto the children of Israel that they go forward, and lift thou up thy rod, and stretch out thine hand over the sea and divide it: and the children of Israel shall go on dry ground through the midst of the sea."(Ex 14:15-16)

When Joshua needed that the light of day should keep on while the Amorites were fighting his people, till his people should win in the battle being waged against them, "Then spake Joshua unto the Lord, "Sun, stand thou still on Gibeon" – and the sun stood still till the Israelites had shown supernal fighting genius to the five kings of the Amorites with their combined armies.

When Ezekiel, worshipper of the Father Almighty raised the dead, he raised a whole valley full.

When the Apostles, worshippers of Sonship Almighty, preached the Risen Christ Jesus, they raised the dead and cured many taken with palsy and lameness.

When worshippers of the Holy Ghost, whom the Father Almighty has sent because of the name of The Second Dispensation, or the Jesus Christ dispensation, do works, they do them on a small scale, but being determinedly related to Universal

Chapter Three – Forgiveness, Affirmation of all as God

Spirit, which is Holy Ghost Influence they sweep the globe with inspiration. For now is come that Great Spirit - the wind in the wings of the messengers of Jehovah-Triumphant - and everywhere the sound as of a mighty wind from heaven.

Has it not been declared that a Breath of Brahma wafts through our common atmospheres, breathable by all who choose to inhale it as strengthening spirit?

The Breath of Brahma was what Job was volitionally inhaling till it healed his mind of grieving and his bones of soreness.

Volitional inspiration or in-breathing of the Heavenly Breath, is sure healing of the mind; sure transformation of our thinking; sure healing of the whole body throughout all its flesh and bones; sure healing of its affairs also.

But who is found indrawing winds his nostrils take no note of, gazing towards a white breath the outer eyes see not? Truly, only those who are revivingly healthy among us have learned that the healing breath never fails, never changes, that it abides for ever in miracle-working competence, exactly as Job reported: "The breath of the Almighty hath given me life."(Job 33:4)

Why, O humankind are you so decrepit, having power to partake of mystical renewal by quickening inspiration? "… ye shall receive power, after that the Holy Ghost is come upon you."(Acts 1:8)

It is the quickening inspiration that wakes the hidden God-Seed: inspiration that cures the mind from thinking; inspiration that draws down the instantaneously working *Ain Soph* above thinking and above being, forgiving the mind of the world, hurrying along the promised speech that distills new health like morning dews.

"With the sounding of the first angel, writes John the Revelator, hail and fire fall, mingled with blood. The first angel is the first call to "Look Up."

Obeying the call, the resistless rule of the skies dissolves opposition with soft *alkahests*. The strain and stressfulness of human existence is hailed upon with blessings from above. A new fervor glows in the speech. The heart fires up with knowledge of a right outshining the law of *Thou shalt not*. The sense of plenitude wakes the shout "All hail sweet riches!" replacing the groan "I want!" This is forgiveness. It is the beauty given for ashes.

When the heart is enlisted, everything we do is prospered. The fire that John saw mingled with hail is the kindled heart.

And the blood that was commingled was the new type of man that is even now already among us, healing and protecting when he appears, as the young man in the furnace protected the three friends of the compassionate king and presented them to him unharmed.

One third of the trees and all the green grass are burnt up by the fire of the new heart and speech. All the competitives that constitute the ginger and glow of human encounter, flourishing like trees for strength, give way to the miracle that sets everyone in their right place. The hastening periods of childhood, youth and old age forego. The man standing in the fiery furnace knows nothing of the seasons of life that are like the grass. Obedience to the mandate: "Look unto Me"(Is 45:22) introduces a new order.

"I will give power to My two watchers" was the promise that John heard from above. (Rev 11:3) This is meant for any two of us who now begin the high watch that woes the God power.

"These are the two olive trees." These are those enriched and set in authority from above, not by effort, not by worthiness, but by restless grace falling over their high watch like the upward visioned Moses and Aaron.

"These are the two candlesticks," priests taught from above, speaking with new tongues needing not that any man should teach them.

"These are the two olive branches," whose golden pipes send forth the golden oil of healing all unseen but resistless as the sky stones called healing hail; the golden oil of enwisdoming till kings know that which they have never read and understand that which they have not been told; the golden oil of prospering till the poor lift up their heads with comfortings, wooed to comrade with those angels who minister cure to poverty. So shall the nations seek and find *Ain Soph*, the Great Countenance above thinking and above being.

With the sounding of the second angel, writes John the Revelator, the sense of personal responsibility, of heavy obligation, rolls softly away. Look up whence the high laws hail, unburdening the tongue of talk of hardship. If the tongue is yet speaking of hardship, its owner has not sensed the second angel's message.

Chapter Three – Forgiveness, Affirmation of all as God

With the sounding of the third angel, the star called *Wormwood* – the mind-preserving principle - wraps the conscious mind in sane security. The mind is forgiven its suggestibility to foolishness and ignorance. It is gathered to Unsuggestible Illumination, *Jehovah-Tsidkenu*, Jehovah our Righteousness.

Until now, all healing has been directed for the benefit of the body or for the lightening of hardship. Now it is that the mind no longer thinks, "I walk on the earth, or on the floor." The mind is cured of such thinking. It gives way to the sight of that foundation under our feet that is God Eternal. The mind is cured of thinking "I put my head upon the pillow." It gives way to seeing underneath the God Arms Everlasting. The mind no longer thinks, "I breathe common atmospheres." It gives way to the glad discovery: "The Spirit of God is in my nostrils," (Job 27:3) and "The Breath of the Almighty has given me life." (Job 44:4)

We always become like those with whom we associate. We are more like the company we keep than that from which we have descended. By association with the *Alkahest* its remitting absoluteness is ours. We associate by converse. Those who communicate with me strengthen, said the Lord of Strength. Those who speak unto me waken. Those who touch me are cured. To them who hold their conversation aright will I show salvation.

The third star was *Wormwood*, or the tonic of divine contagion. "Repent, for the remission, and ye shall feel the contagion," (Mk 1:4, Lk 3:3) said Peter to the brethren. Repenting himself, he caught the curing contagions. "Now let signs and wonders be wrought!" he shouted. "By stretching forth thine hand, to heal, O God!" (Acts 4:30), as the curing flakes fell even upon his shadow.

"Hurt not the oil and the wine," cried the angel of the third seal. Hurt not the doctrine of denial, the cathartic oil of unburdening recognition and its speech as, "Facing Thee, there is neither sickness nor death on my pathway." Hurt not the strengthening wine of affirmation, as "There is none beside Thee." "Thou hast forgiven my mind."

"My bark is wafted from the strand by breath divine and on the helm there rests a hand other than mine."

"The third, the face of a lion," writes the entranced Ezekiel. (Ezek 10:14) The lion is the emblem of strength, sovereignty, and princely achievement. We are as strong, as sovereign, as able, as our backing, our consort, our *aide-de-camp*. "I can build a house!" shouts the tiny child clinging to his father's hand. He feels the strength of his father. We feel the Strength of our Father-God, when clinging to His Hand.

It has been prophesied that by association with angels, we shall know new music, new architecture, and new laws of life.

And the third stone in the foundation of character is the chalcedony. The chalcedony is copper-emerald, strength by associating with Strength; and sky-tinted opal, emblem of circumambient quenchless life. Now have I bitten off a leaf from the tree of Immortality. Now have I partaken of Eternity's Reviving Breath! Now am I wise with high inspiration!

"Fortify thy power by the contagion of Power," preached Nahum. He was proclaiming contagion, or for-giveness, beginning at the self, or Jerusalem, seven hundred years before the undestroyable Christ gave orders to declare strength for weakness and life for death, beginning at *The Self* or Jerusalem.

As the needle is nerved with magnetic power by communing with the magnet, so are we nerved with God-power by converse with the *I Am That I Am*, Author of Omnipotence.

Thy lamp of hastening Omniscience shines newly on my liberated brain.

Preach the gospel, heal the sick, cast out demoniac dispositions, and raise the dead. Welcome the contagion of All-Efficiency. Behold, God exalts by His Power; who teaches like Him. Making the great surrender, Spirit Almighty acts in our behalf.

We can imbue with peace by recognizing the ever-presence of Everlasting Peace. We can separate ourselves unto any one force, or energy, or attribute, and by persevering attention to it, can become the embodiment of it.

Now is the time for us to choose the power, or force, or energy, we would embody in ourselves, and make essay at it till all its characteristics are ours, and the efficiency that lies in it is our efficiency. Is it not written, "The works that I do, ye shall do also."(Jn 14:12)

"Sing and rejoice, O daughter of Zion! For lo, I come, and will dwell in the midst of thee," said the Lord. (Is 52:2) Let us choose to be identified with the Lord, Strong and Mighty. The Lord who is able to keep us from falling, whose is the kingdom, the power and the glory. For our contagion, we will separate unto "the Great, the Mighty God, great in counsel and mighty to work."(Jer 32:18, Is 28:29)

The Lord Unknowable All-Knowing, originates all knowing. The Intense, Inane All-Power, is the Author of all activity. The Mystical Stillness wakes tongues. Is it not written, "I will give you a mouth and wisdom, which all your adversaries shall not be able to gainsay?"(Lk 21:15)

Was not Stephen charged with Spirit so that he wrought spiritual miracles? Did not Peter speak with resistless eloquence to the converting of three thousand people in one day? Thus have the Real mystics of all time been tongues of fire.

Every objective to which we give our attention has its storage of possibilities ready to spring forth and proceed *in extenso* through its devotee.

Mind follows the visional sense. Hannah's grieved mind was suddenly transformed to joyous proclamations of the glory of living, and to praise of the prayer-answering God. But it had taken years of her obedience to the mandate of the forgiving Presence to have this sudden trans-substantiation by contagion of Divinity.

Jahaziel had elected to identify with Miracle-Working Spirit, and at the battle with the Ammonites he proclaimed that the Jews need not try to defend themselves for the Lord would fight for them. Like Hannah, he had come to the day of Fulfillment.

The poet-scholar Leopardi taught mankind that a pitiless nature has man at its mercy. By this election his life, mind, and affairs were chased by poverty, despair and illness.

These are demonstrations on the blackboard of existence. They prove the transmuting energy resident in all objectives. They prove that what we now experience we need experience no longer.

Our weakness waits transmuting for-giveness. Our ignorance stays with us until our vision toward the Author of Omniscience comes to us with our own right knowledge. Come, gather to Him ever near, who for-gives us altogether, so that we find ourselves holding our conversation aright – "O Thou hast for-given myself with Thyself!"

Chapter Three – Forgiveness, Affirmation of all as God

There is unspoken wisdom awaiting our separation unto the Giver of Wisdom. There is imperturbable health awaiting our separation unto the Imperturbable Author of Health. There is authority over the transactions of daily encounter by separation unto the Unconditioned and Absolute. With right glance and with right speech, we superintend the animate and inanimate. We shall be poor no more, if we separate ourselves unto the Owner, Chief Presence in the universe.

We always become receptive, soft, and plastic, to that objective unto which we oftenest give our inner eye. "God makes my heart soft," said Job, the devotee to God. (Job 23:16) "But at the end of the days I lifted up mine eyes unto heaven and mine understanding returned unto me – and at the same time my reason returned unto me; and mine honor and brightness returned unto me." (Dan 4:34-36)

A sensitive photographic film steadily exposed to the night skies takes imprint of stars, which the telescope cannot discover. So those who become sensitive, through steadfast attention to the Wisdom-Countenance ever shining upon them, know laws which the books have not recorded. They show forth activities never recorded in history. "My servant shall deal prudently, he shall be exalted and extolled, and be very high." (Is 52:13) This is the result of much attention to the High and Lofty One inhabiting Eternity.

To become sufficiently sensitive, receptive, and tender to an objective is to be its servant, doing its will. "I came down from heaven not to do my own will, but the will of Him that sent me."(Jn 6:38) This was the secret of the heroism of the Redeemer. You cannot be receptive to two opposites at the same time, was His science.

The triumphing *I AM*, is not vitally promulgated by us, because we have been receptive, sensitive, tender to the non-triumphing opposite to the *I AM*. "Behold Me, behold Me all the day long."(Is 65:1) Only Thee mayest heal me Thou most Glorious Manthra Spenta."

In the days when the proud opposites to the Great Fact have rule, shall the King of Kings be chosen – was Isaiah's view of this moment. When *"Labor omnia vincit"* is the motto of men, "Labor not" shall be the risen watchword, "Take no thought" shall be the law. In the days when hospitals are most beloved by reason of their agreement with the destructible opposite, the inhabitants shall stop saying, "I am sick," and the angels shall save all feet from stumbling.

In the days when nations are leaning upon their armies, "Put up thy sword" shall be obeyed. While prisons are yawning for criminals, "Neither hath this man sinned

Chapter Three – Forgiveness, Affirmation of all as God

nor his parents" shall everywhere be declared true of all people, every eye on the uninjurable Soul Self fathered by Jehovah The Glorious.

While money is the substance most desired, for which kings and scholars are bartering their titles, the sensitive to divine Substance shall "cast their silver in the streets, and their gold shall be removed."

While scholarship is at its highest pitch of repute, people shall rise taught of God the things that the schools discuss not.

Neither shall the powers and capacities of mind be science. "The righteousness of the righteous shall not save him, nor the wickedness of the wicked destroy him," touches a tonic chord of the miracle above thinking and its resultant conduct. God enthroned above the pairs of opposites is "the bad man's deliverer and the good man's glorious liberty."

Thou shall be hid from the scourge of the silent and audible tongue," strikes beyond the range of human effort.

The watchers for iniquity shall be cut off, that make someone an offender for a word," shows a rule of relationship transcending criticism.

"Take no thought." "Lift up your eyes," is Christian mysticism.

"What I say unto you, I say unto all, Watch," is Jesus Christ magism.

"I have a way that no fowl knows and which the vulture's eye has not seen," says the Rewarder of the diligently watchful. The "fowl" is the looker for right words and their outcomes. The "vulture" is the searcher for sin and its consequences. This was the patience and the faith of the saints of old, the observers of badness and goodness, the strong believers in rewards and punishments, the unknowing of the law of what you see, that too become you must.

Until the High Redeemer, inhabiting Eternity, is made the objective of the all-achieving visional sense, those who take the sword must perish by the sword. They who lead into captivity must be led captive, and no power can ward off the victims' exactness of duplication for all the time the mystic law is printing on life and mind and body, the inner eye's telltale intaglios or engravings.

Chapter Three – Forgiveness, Affirmation of all as God

The One served by inward beholding gives for our former nature Its own Nature. Converse with angelic spirits etherealizes the body and turns it, by degrees, into Soul's Divine Essence. Some seem to be on fire during their prayers to the Supernal Presence.

Today there are those who, by contemplating the Healing God, rather than their own pains, have been given for their diseased bodies, vigorously healthy ones. For their depressed minds, they have been given buoyancy of heart, thus bodily preaching forgiveness.

The thing we fear is the objective our inward beholding touches with contagion. Lightning, drought, miasma, loss, deprivation, and sickness – they soon find lodgment, embodiment, and expression in us.

"Oh! Why will ye die?" cried the Hebrew prophets. Can you not read the divine decree, "Look unto Me and be ye saved?"(Is 45:22) There is a ground of ready affiliation in our constitution, in which the germs of contagion find strong root – God if we contagion God; misery if we contagion misery.

Jesus of Nazareth had no consenting ground of affiliation with satanic cowardice, feebleness, or inefficiency. He said that evil could find nothing to tie to in Him. The ground He had kept was sensitive to the Ruler in the heavens and the earth, so that He could speak forth from experiential evidence: "All power is given unto me in heaven and in earth."(Matt 28:18) Where I am, there ye may be also."(Jn 14:3)

He urged to preach for-giveness, to teach humanity to stand and feed in the strength of the Almighty. He taught them to breathe in the Almighty; to wake the God-Seed by vision, by breath; for the inspiration of the Almighty awakens understanding, stirs the God.

Agree with the One God who is Adversary to pain, misfortune, and defeat. Agree with this Adversary quickly – now! "Behold I am against thee,"(Jer 21:13) says the Highest Lord…I am against your feasts… even your solemn meetings.

We feed on what we inwardly behold. We see the saving Substance that our neighbors might feast upon by lifting up their eyes to the fields white for harvest, but we cannot make them look and taste. Our neighbors know that our vision is Truth, but they obey not.

Long ago the Parsees had already proclaimed that nine-hundred ninety-nine thousand, nine-hundred ninety-nine diseases spring from low visioning; but that when the most Glorious Highest is being sought, the diseases should all fall away.

"The ransomed return with singing."(Is 35:10) They reach joy by affiliating with the Author of joy. The taste of joy gives a sense of success with a new leverage. The deaf man who spoke with passionate earnestness to the Presence of God in the Universe, felt a great cleavage in his head, and blood flowed forth from his ears. The gates of his imprisoned hearing being opened, he shouted for joy. The kingdom of heaven comes and finds something to tie to in those who touch the God-estimates. Knowing meets knowing.

Honor, fortune, and knowledge are for-giveness by recognition of the Glorious Presence of Victorious Divinity. Health, strength, joy, and peace cooperate as God with man, by upward visioning.

We find new knowing by upward viewing toward the Author of knowing. New knowing starts with mystically sighting toward the Original Knower, by whom our knowing roots are quickened. Let us know from our own base, then poverty and foolishness and evil have nothing to tie to. Thus do we find our original good. So are we for-given.

Paul called the day of joy the day of atonement. "We joy in God through Jesus Christ, by whom, (accepting our sonship), as he declared we have now received the atonement." (Rom 5:11) Jesus called it the day of for-giveness. To the man let down through the roof, all calloused with misery, he said "For-given." To the woman bruised of heart, he said "For-given." And thus were these both brought to conviction – not of sin, but of Sonship.

Agreement is harmony. And harmony with the Adversary to pain, ignorance, and disorder, means success like the Adversary. I will contend with them that contend with thee. He that strikes at you strikes at me. You are My servant, fear not. They that war against you shall be as naught."(Is 41:12) "O, I Thou, and Thou I!"

High success denotes entire harmony, entire for-giveness. Those who are entirely for-given speak with resistless inspiration. They have the heavenly hearthfire. They are world kindlers. No opposition daunts them. Life, health, and joy are eternally native to them.

Chapter Three – Forgiveness, Affirmation of all as God

The third angel's burning lamp is the speech of the Imperturbable Knower. It is mind tonic, wormwood to the vitals – ware-mood - mind-preserving acquaintance with the Presence of the Healing Christ.

"He that humbles himself shall be exalted."(Lk 14:11, 18:14) They who let themselves go to the Finished Fact, as the inconsequent needle yields to the magnet's empowering, are new characters on the earth. By their utter meekness, they are liberated from themselves, and do the works of the Worker unto whom they have yielded themselves.

The Sacred Books, uttering the inspiration of the God-taught, lay great stress on voluntary surrender to the Divine Trend. "Put on humbleness, meekness."(Col 3:12) "Because you heart was tender and you did humble yourself before God…behold I will gather you. "If my people shall humble themselves, I will for-give …and heal all their land"

You shall walk prosperously because of meekness."(II Chr 34:27)

It was while Daniel was voluntarily casting himself down, to be taken possession of by the Saving Sovereignty in the Universe, that the angel being caused to fly, touched him with heavenly inspiration and said, "Ho Daniel! I am come to give you skill and understanding. Stand upright on your feet."

We gladly offer the sum total of our unlikeness to the Almighty Giver. We gladly offer the initiation fee of our contrary tempers at the courts of the Healing God.

The third angel's voice wakes the will to let go the last vestige of opposition to the Mighty Trend. What matter how unlike to *our* way is *The Way* our life seems to be moving? We take with us words and return, looking steadfastly unto the Great Mover. Is it not assured that when the Lord returns our returning, our mouth is filled with laughter, and our tongue with singing?

How else than by being free inspiration can we warm the world into health? How else than by being God-glowing can we go into all the world, preaching the gospel and raising the dead? How else than by High Association can we contagion free inspiration, the Holy Spirit influence that sweeps down all aftermath of low visioning?

Chapter Three – Forgiveness, Affirmation of all as God

Some sages have touched the law hymned by the third angel: "Bow down to me and you shall come even to Me... Take sanctuary with Me alone and I shall liberate you from all sin by the resplendent Lamp of Wisdom."

Milton immortalized his acquaintance with the Third Star's supernal import: "What is dark in me illumine. What is low raise and support, that to the height of the great argument I may assert Eternal providence, and justify the ways of God to man."

The all-conquering Jesus passed through the gates of voluntary lowliness, and taught us all that identifying worship, when it touches the conquering truth, has come up out of the baptismal font of humility. "God is Spirit: and they that worship Him, must worship Him in the spirit *of humility* and in *the bold words* of truth."(Jn 4:24)

Now we are ready to cast ourselves and all our wills and demands in lowly yielding up to the Unseen High Sovereignty and His own Providence. "Who is not glad to surrender his proud mind's muddy puddles of foolishness, its dark pools of ignorance?"

Here is my mind; I spread it out before Thee. For-give Thou its foolishness and ignorance with Thy Bright Wisdom.

Here is my life impulsion; I offer it to Thee. For-give thou all its contrariness to Thee.

Here is my heart; it is Thine only. For-give Thou its dissatisfactions; for-give its restlessness. For-give its discouragements; for-give its elations. For-give its hopes and its fears, its loves and its hates.

Here is my body I cast it down before Thee. For-give Thou its imperfections with Thy Perfection. For-give me altogether with Thyself.

So only can I be the life and inspiration of the five bold words of Truth – Hymns to the eternal glowing Virgins with oil of healing and oil of illumination in their everlasting lamps.

Thou art and there is none beside Thee, in Thine own Omnipresence, Omnipotence, and Omniscience.

Chapter Three – Forgiveness, Affirmation of all as God

I am Thine only and in Thee I live, move and have my being.

I am Thine own Substance, Power and Light, and I shed abroad wisdom, strength, and holiness from Thee.

Thou art now working through me to will and to do that which ought to be done by me.

I am for-given and governed by Thee alone, and I cannot sin, I cannot suffer for sin, nor fear sin, sickness, or death.

My soul, doing obeisance unto the Wonder of Thee, wakes again these hymns of the Morning Stars in praise of Thee.

High praise of Him - all Forgiveness - draws to us the promised New Language. It brings into view the New Race to be sent down from heaven foreseen by the keepers of the five hymns that should some time "sing-in" the Golden Age.

Practice

Bible verses to commit to memory.

> ➤ "There is forgiveness with Thee."(Ps 130:4)
>
> ➤ "To the Lord our God belongs forgiveness."(Dan 9:9)
>
> ➤ "If my people, upon whom my name is called, shall humble themselves, and seek my face, and turn from their wicked ways; then will I hear from heaven, and will forgive all the land."(II Chr 3:12)
>
> ➤ "He that humbleth himself shall be exhalted." (Lk 14:11)
>
> ➤ "Put on humbleness of mind, and meekness." (Col 3:12)
>
> ➤ "Because thine heart was tender, and thou didst humble thyself before God - I have even heard thee also," saith the Lord. (II Chr 34:27)
>
> ➤ "Behold, my servant shall prosper, he shall be exalted and extolled, and be very high."(Is 52:13)

Chapter Three – Forgiveness, Affirmation of all as God

> "Who forgiveth all thine iniquities, who healeth all thy diseases." (Ps 103:3)

Résumé – Wednesday- First Week

If nothing hurts Free Spirit and I am Free Spirit, unhurt forever – I have something given for the imagination of hurting which has now slipped away from me. This that takes the place of hurts is Beauty, Joy, Praise, and Wholeness.

Preach forgiveness, or the given-for. "I will greatly rejoice in the Lord, my soul shall be joyful in my God; for he hath clothed me with the garments of salvation. He hath covered me with the robe of righteousness, as a bridegroom decks himself with ornaments, and as a bride adorns herself with her jewels. For as the earth brings forth her bud, and as the garden causes the things that are sown in it to spring forth; so the Lord God will cause righteousness and praise to spring forth before all the nations."(Is 61:10-11)

As the needle can become a magnet by rubbing against a magnet, so we can do God-works by closely relating ourselves to the Healer of all diseases, the Redeemer from destruction, the Great in Counsel. As the needle must utterly yield herself so must we utterly yield ourselves. We must have our eye single to One Only - to be full of that One Only. Utter yielding is called "meekness," in the Scriptures.

There is a Divine Fiat ever going forth. There is a Divine Providence always acting. If we hold the magnetic needle still, it is restless until it is free to point north. So we are restless under the cramps formulated by our own visioning toward evil, or the body of matter, of pain and decay. These slough off with the high watch and the shouts of the free. We sense the Divine Providence—the Heavenly Fiat. The sense of the kind and good and joy-giving Providence up-bearing us forever has been called the *Cosmic Consciousness*. Its ecstasy of rest in the Lord has been called *forgiveness*.

Great Proclamations have issued forth from those who have experienced the cosmic consciousness, or forgiveness. These proclamations have been called *Affirmations of Eternal Truth*. They have been called *Hymns to the Eternal*. They have been figuratively spoken of as *Wise Virgins*, with oil of healing and oil of illuminating in their influence.

The needle cannot attract like a magnet if it does not yield itself *in toto*, to the magnet. So it is that no one can be the embodiment of the five eternal proclamations, unless they have let their mind, their life, their heart, and their body, go free to the winds of the Divine Fiat. They must first look up often to the Sun of

Chapter Three – Forgiveness, Affirmation of all as God

Righteousness with healing in his wings. "There is none beside Thee." (I Chr 17:20) "The Lord shall judge the ends of the earth; and he shall give strength unto his king, and exalt the horn of his anointed."(I Sam 2:10)

A young man volitionally offered himself to the Stream of Divine Order, letting go of himself like a reed in the wind, fully expecting annihilation. To his surprise he found his bad habits gone, his despair dissolved, his character and body strengthened and his whole being infused with radiance.

The risen Christ taught volitional meekness, volitional offering: "He that humbles himself shall be exalted."(Luke 14:11)

Let us take Wednesday to voluntarily offer ourselves to the King of Kings and Lord of Lords. They that worship in meekness are the ready harp strings for the divine melodies of the five hymns of praise – the five proclamations of truth. They are the voicing of instruments of health and quickening life.

Here again is the form of voluntary surrender of self in meekness and the full text of all the illuminative sayings for centuries, whenever people have found themselves yielding in humility and rising up for-given:

Here is my mind; I spread it out before Thee. For-give Thou its foolishness and ignorance with Thy Bright Wisdom.

Here is my life impulsion; I offer it to Thee. For-give thou all its contrariness to Thee.

Here is my heart; it is Thine only. For-give Thou its dissatisfactions; for-give its restlessness. For-give its discouragements; for-give its elations. For-give its hopes and its fears, its loves and its hates.

Here is my body I cast it down before Thee. For-give Thou its imperfections with Thy Perfection. For-give me altogether with Thyself.

So only can I be the life and inspiration of the five bold words of Truth – Hymns to the eternal glowing Virgins with oil of healing and oil of illumination in their everlasting lamps.

Chapter Three – Forgiveness, Affirmation of all as God

Thou art and there is none beside Thee, in Thine own Omnipresence, Omnipotence, and Omniscience.

I am Thine only and in Thee I live, move and have my being.

I am Thine own Substance, Power and Light, and I shed abroad wisdom, strength, and holiness from Thee.

Thou art now working through me to will and to do that which ought to be done by me.

I am for-given and governed by Thee alone, and I cannot sin, I cannot suffer for sin, nor fear sin, sickness, or death.

"Bow down thyself to me and thou shalt come even to me. Take sanctuary with me alone and I shall liberate you from all sin, by the Resplendent Lamp of Wisdom" - Vedic Hymn

With the experience of for-giveness, or the Hestia Vestia of bold Truth, John foresees a star called, "Wormwood," falling to the earth. (Rev 8:10) A "star" is a great character. And "wormwood" is mind preserver, or mind cure. One shall be the embodiment of Truth so inspiringly that he shall cure the world mind of its earth-drowse.

When someone is sick or in pain he is in telluric slumber or earth-drowse. He is magnetized by foolishness and ignorance. His mind is thrilled by foolishness and ignorance: earth-sleep.

John the Revelator sees one to arise all awake. His vivid sense of Living Spirit shall kindle in humanity, now asleep, the vivid sense of Living Spirit, of the giving for matter's laws the law of the Spirit of life in Jesus Christ.

Chapter Four – Faith, the Evidence that God is All

Thursday, First Week

4th Gate - **I do believe that the true God is now working with me and through me and by me and for me, to make me a living demonstration of omnipresent, omnipotent, omniscient goodness.**

This fourth Study has treatment quality for all who read it, even though they may not have heard its subject matter discussed orally. Practicing its lordly formulas wakes victorious energies.

-a-

Every number held profound significance to the ancients. Number four held the fire of convincing energy. It was the Uriel angel of divine telepathy. The sparkling up of our faith center is the awakening of our hidden miracle-working genius. Number four is a sign of the fertile square, the touch of fourth dimensional strength.

The fourth stone, symbolic of character, according to St. John of the Revelation, is the emerald. It was once thought to hold radiations for sharpening the memory, even to the recalling of our heavenly beginnings, making us mindful of "that country whence we came out," a country to which all may return.

Not in entire forgetfulness, but trailing clouds of glory do we come from God who is our Home.

Everything about four was fourth dimensional to the wise men of old. Notice them telling how man is comraded by angels from the city of God when he finds himself touching the fourth side of the city that lies four square.

Things have never satisfied the seat of our sacred starvation – nor yet noble thoughts, or high statements, even the highest. Only by laying hold of the High Adequate have we laid hold on that which satisfies the heart's desire. Notice the wise men telling of Jacob by the Jabbok brook sensing the angel of God who called himself God, changing him from Jacob the frightened to Israel, the fearless, and causing him to found a dynasty of kings ending in earth's final King – The Nazarene Jesus!

Chapter Four – Faith, the Evidence that God is All

The phoenix bird which fell into helpless ashes and rose into winged majesty was once the symbol of humanity's helplessness in the face of death, rising into daring renewal above death by the sacred touch of heaven's Uriel fire on his yearning heart's despair. Not only did the phoenix signify survival after death but revival out of death.

As the mariner on the sea steers his ship's course by a needle which points to a magnetic north, so we are truly steering our hopes by an inner needle pointing to a country unseen from whence miraculous succor may swing toward us in time of danger or despair.

Something within us innately hopes great things from the self-existent kingdom. "Mine eyes are ever toward the Lord, for he shall pluck my feet out of the net."(Ps 25:15)

David was rewarded for his bold insistence, his persistent high watch – "I went through fire and water," he cried, "but thou broughtest me out into a wealthy place." (Ps 18:19)

It was the business of the Levitical singers in David's time and in Solomon's time to sing the ways of the kingdom unseen in its miraculous workings with this visible world and its people. "Thou shalt ride prosperously because of meekness," they chanted to the high-pitched, rich-toned, sackbut of many strings. (Ps 45:4)

David had been meek even to sorrowing daily in his heart before the Lord of his hope who seemed sometimes to hide His face from him. Therefore was the promise fulfilled upon him. "Thou shalt ride prosperously because of meekness." "I will sing unto the Lord because he hath dealt bountifully with me," (Ps 13:6) he proclaimed triumphantly.

As a lighted candle lights another, so conviction fires conviction. We rise up with that authority before which we have been meek. Was Isaiah not meek before the Lord of hosts until the Lord of hosts told him to command the Lord of Hosts as an Obedient Servitor? Was Jeremiah not meek before the Ruler in the heavens and the earth until the Ruler in the heavens and the earth told him to show himself ruler over the nations and over the kingdoms?

Did Jesus not mean, "Have the Rulership of God Himself," when He told His disciples to have the faith of God? For is faith not rulership? Is faith not kingship, confidence, or command? Is kingship not always associated with confidence to command? "If ye have faith as a grain of mustard seed, ye shall say unto this mountain: remove hence to yonder place; and it shall remove: and nothing shall be impossible to you."(Matt 17:20)

Peter wrote that angels, authorities and powers are subject to the hidden power of the heart; the waiting Authority Principle lingering in the being of every man, woman or child on earth.

The mystery of obedience to authority is manifest every instant. Do we not have to obey the authority of the doorknob before it works for us? Or have to obey the rigid law of our feet before they do what we wish of them? So the Mighty King we call God gives orders to which we must yield obedience before His sublime service in our behalf is sublimely manifest. "The Lord lifteth up the meek..." (Ps 147:6) He lifts up those who are gently receptive to burning God conviction which is the confidence to command - which is kingship ever waiting to find its meek sparkling tinder within us.

It is practicing inborn native kingship to utter bold commands going about the world saying to the lame "Walk!" and they walk. Or saying to the deaf, "Hear!" and they hear. But no one can tell us like the Hebrew prophets and the masterful Nazarene the practice that rouses the living dominance called by Peter the hidden man of the heart, our secret *Jehovah Nissi* – Jehovah, my banner.

Jesus and the prophets teach us to be insistent and firm with the Waiting Adequate who is most willing and competent. "Is anything too hard for Me?"(Gen 18:14) "Hast thou faith? Have it to thyself before God." "Lo, I am with you always." (Matt 28:20) "For the Lord shall be thy confidence, and shall keep thy foot from being taken." (Prov 3:26) "Concerning the works of my hands command ye me." (Is 45:11)

Note how universal God majesty awaits the rise of human majesty universal!

Joseph in the prison house of Egypt's Pharaoh was meek to the fulfillment of the prophecy that he should save the Jews from starvation. He stopped his own thinking until the Unseen Knower touched his brain with divine wisdom and words not known by anyone on earth. So great Pharaoh set him over all the provinces of the realm and gave him the handling of all the gold and silver of the realm. Joseph rose to kingly authority because he was touched with sprinklings of gray matter from above until his speech did distill as the dew.

Chapter Four – Faith, the Evidence that God is All

We find that the people, who have been baptized with originality, have let the world's thinking alone, and have let go even of their own thinking - so creative new knowledge has been free to touch them. This is the magic wisdom of Jesus of Nazareth: "Take no thought" – "In such an hour as ye think not."(Lk 12:40)

Even in print we read how some clergymen admit catching their thoughts from the thoughts of their congregations. So they are not original in their instructions. The world now needs fresh news from Universal Wisdom, new distillations from Divine Beneficence, sparkling gray matter drops charged with healing from on high.

Jesus discussed the mystery of forgiveness. He proved the mystery of bold use of the Working Executive facing us through all things, ever saying: "Boldly tell Me what to do and when to act."(Eph 6:20)

"Prosper Thou me!" commanded King David. "Prosperity is of Thee." "The silver and the gold are Thine," "Riches and honor come of Thee."

Such truthful recognitions caused plenteousness of gold and silver to come to him exactly as such truthful recognitions would now cause plenteousness to come to any one of earth's multitudinous children of the Highest. By this fourth lesson with its grand offerings, we see that Deity is no disciplinarian giving us hardships, but a Beneficent Presence awaiting our use of the everywhere facing Beneficence by bold insistence. "Glorify thou me."(Jn 17:15) "Prosper thou me." "Answer thou me."(Job 38:3) "Stand thou still."(Ex 14:13, Numb 9:8, Job 37:14)

"Come boldly up," said Paul. Why not come boldly up if "boldness has genius, power and magic in It?"

This One everywhere and through everything facing us, is no *hound of heaven*, hounding us to starvation, cold, or death. Neither are we His hound dogs beaten into submission to His ceaseless discipline. Let us take right view of Him: "Ask what ye will," (Jn 15:7) "Concerning the works of my hands, command ye Me," (Is 45:11) "Is anything too hard for Me?" (Gen 18:14) "I will work, and none shall hinder."(I Sam 14:6)

Speak boldly, looking to the face of the answering Substance, "Deliver Thou me from evil!" "Give me this day my super-substantial bread!" "Give me courage, confidence to insist! Bless me with life, wisdom, and divine efficiency!"(Matt 6: 9-13)

Chapter Four – Faith, the Evidence that God is All

This recognition picks up the formulating substance and translates it into the mystic's fulfilled assurance - So shall thy life renew; so shall inspiration teach thee; so shall thy affairs go newly right with thee.

We light our inner vision by exalting it. Lightened vision wakes all our faculties to sense the Supernal Good-Willing surrounding us, forever wooing our positive high watch. Give me for my weakness, strength to command Thee!

Some things will never square right with humanity till it takes Deity at His word, "Command ye Me." (Is 45:11)

Stop talking about God and His idea of humanity, and speak unto majestic Deity face to face! So shall majestic humanity arise, victoriously daring! "Bow down thine ear to me; deliver me speedily."(II Kings 19:16, Ps 17:6) "Thy gentleness hath made me great."(Ps 18:35)

-b-

As Adam and Eve were not only individuals but perceptions, so are the Angels of the Apocalypse not only winged messengers but high perceptions and their activities.

The Egyptian Magi changed the name of the neophyte at the fourth perception, because at this his nature changed. From being a meek listener he became a bold speaker; from being a timid follower he became a daring leader.

The fourth angel smites one side of the sun and on that side it is dark. So did the same angel smite Jacob and one side of him was withered, not for use but for super-use. So did this mighty angel smite Peter in the prison, and the smitten side of him being now supernal perception and not common intelligence, even as Angels of the Free Adequate, opened the bolted prison doors and undid the chains and manacles that human animosity had welded. The Roman soldiers guarding him four quaternions strong were smitten, and the miracle proceeded onward uninterrupted.

The fourth perception, setting aside common law, exposes the unmanageable fourth dimension in space, which makes locks and bars and lions' teeth and adverse criticisms of no account.

Job the stricken was searching for help with his watch toward heaven, when suddenly he sensed the fourth dimension, and life for him became a track of victorious light to lighten all generations after him.

Chapter Four – Faith, the Evidence that God is All

Jacob sensed the presence of the angel of the miracle, the angel of the helping, and wrestled with the angel, enduring as seeing the invisible, and his name was changed to Israel. He was no longer Jacob the cringeling, but Israel, the Prince whom God Himself served. To any daring wrestler with the everpresent angel of the miracle anyone may hear that Angel Servant responding, "Concerning the work of My hands, command ye Me." (Is 45:11) "As a prince thou hast power with God."

At the fourth perception David found the same servant: "Bow down Thine ear to me; deliver me speedily," he cried. "Thy gentleness has made me great," (2 Sam 22:36) was his astonished acknowledgment.

At his fourth perception, Isaiah implores all humanity to practice the formula of the fourth dimension, whether they themselves have been entranced by the fourth angels' smiting or not. "Thus says the Lord, Ask Me of things to come, and concerning the works of My hands, command ye Me." (Is 45:11)

Jesus the Redeemer gave the formula of the fourth verbatim. It is the speech of the fundamental knower risen up out of the waters of humility. It is the speech of the hidden being of the heart, without age or nationality.

It is the genius of Massini at seventy singing Gounod's "Sanctus" to an enthralled congregation. It is the genius of Elman at seventeen drawing a magic bow across a magic instrument to enraptured throngs. How thirstily the people put their lips to the troughs where living waters flow! What hearts of love they lean close to fires celestial!

The entire world travails for the fourth angel's birthmark – the parting of its common mind for its uncircumscribed genius to act. "Who is it that comes from Edom with dyed garments from Bozrah? I that speak in brightness, mighty to save." I that have dyed my language in the word of the High Supernal. I that have dipped my will in the Heavenly Trend . I smitten by the angel of the miracle and his delivering might. "Arise up, quickly!" the angel says. Now am I as Jacob, not for visible but for mystical usefulness. Now am I as Peter, free Spirit.

A principle is a comprehensive law or doctrine from which others are derived. That is, obedience is vested in the Supreme I AM.

Something concerning the mystery of humanity's inborn authority has ever been the fourth theme of those who have consciously or unwittingly obeyed the Supreme edict, "Look unto Me." By snatches of what Luke the Apostle called sunrisings from on high, the illuminati of the ages have known that the will to command the Obedient Supreme Presence rises up after obedience to the will of the Supreme Presence.

The law is plain enough. If that nature before which we have been negative or receptive, soft, meek, plastic, draws forth and stirs alive in us its own kind, it is not surprising that the meekest and lowliest of all men rose up with the bold proclamation: "All power is given unto me"(Matt 28:18) "I have overcome the world."(Jn 16:33) It is not surprising that his disciples, catching his assurance, found that satanic tempers fled at the sound of their bold commands, and the willing angel of the miracle stood by them to save them from prisons and swords.

Tell ye the daughter of Zion, behold, kingship cometh in meekness. This is Zechariah agreeing with Jesus across the gulf of centuries. The mystic law is one and its way is one as mathematics is one.

Jesus gladly sacrificed Himself to call the attention of humanity to the root of Divinity, the spark of identical substance with the Unconditioned Absolute inherent in each and all.

With Jesus came the time for showing the root of divine authority bone of bone in humanity for ever, in their relation to the Supreme Good Will occupying Omnipresence: "Thus says the Holy One of Israel, concerning the work of My hands, command ye Me" (Is 45:11). Therefore after this manner pray ye: "Give me this day my super-substantial bread – bread for my eternally innate authority with the God that stands in the congregation of the Universe!"

Jesus, the Bloom in the Garden of Man, rising up out of authority-breeding lowliness told us to speak like masters to the responsive stately God of Lazarus; to the stately responsive God of the man with the impotent arm. Speak boldly to the stately responsive God of the mountain and to the obedient responsive sycamore tree.

Speak in this manner: "Thy kingdom come!"(Matt 6:10) "Thine is the Kingdom forever!" (Matt 6:13) "Stretch forth thy hand!"(Matt 12:13, Mk 3:5, Lk 6:10) "Make straight the path!"(Is 40:3) His God did not over-discipline man. His God awaited man's bold insistence, "Make straight my path!"

This is the rise of the Hidden Man of Job, of Joshua, of Jacob – the great triumvirate of J's on the commanding heights of courage to command the willing

Omnipotence ever whispering to all humanity "Concerning the work of My hand, command ye Me!" (Is 45:11)

Did not Job hear the Supreme Authority in heaven and earth speaking with sternness, "I will demand of thee and answer thou Me" – over and over, till the intone of it smote his root of divinity, and he turned with the same address, "I will demand of Thee, and answer Thou me!" And is it not recorded that the Lord was pleased with Job? (Job 38:3)

Was it not to the Lord fronting him through the sun and moon that Joshua spake with bold commanding, "Sun, stand thou still on Gibeon, and thou moon in the valley of Ajalon! And the sun stood still in the midst of the heavens, and hasted not to go down about a whole day. And there was no day like that, when Joshua spake unto the Lord." (Jos 10:12) With the rise of his inborn Root of authority spake he to the Willing Obedience facing him as the Omnipotent One.

And did not Jacob wrestle to give his hidden boldness dominion? "I will not let Thee go except Thou bless me!" (Gen 32:26) And the yielding Angel of Victory did vouchsafe the blessing. "I have seen God face to face," said the transmuted Jacob. I was afraid, but fear had no annulling strength against my vision of God.

We must choose well the objective before which our inner eye oftenest pauses. If the objective has not commanding boldness and resistless authority as its savor, commanding boldness and resistless authority will not rise up out of its sleeping place in us when the moment of identification transpires.

Gather a hint from the slow rising Moses, docile, teachable, tractable, before the tutors of princes famed for their learning and manners. Is it not written in secular history that Moses also was famed for his learning and manners? But at forty years of age he fled like a cringing Jacob at the threats of the Israelites. No confidence to command and be obeyed had leaped like a fountain of fire from its slumbering pit in him. How could it, if the tutors to whom he had been religiously attentive had never waked their own fearless dominion? Can a stream rise higher than its source?

Now exiled among the mountains of Midian, he has spent forty years humbling himself before the High Deliverer, the Noble Counselor, the Almighty Champion, and though he is eighty years of age two million Israelites obey his lightest word of command. Notice the mathematical increase, afraid of two, dominant over two million! The Lord of Lords and Ruler of the Heavens and the earth sends him forth Law giver, Governor, Mighty Champion, High Deliverer like Himself. He sends him

Chapter Four – Faith, the Evidence that God is All

forth with youth in his genius, the stamp of Fadelessness on his body. "Here eyes do regard you in Eternity's stillness: choose well, your choice is brief and yet endless."

"Let the Lord be thy confidence, he will not suffer thy feet to be taken."(Prov 3:26) This is the principle of attention to the Highest Lord and leads to the point of rising above prisons and lions' jaws. This is the principle of making them of no effect. The lordship that causes the iron gates to open of their own accord, that rolls away the stones from the pathway, must hail from above the three dimensions.

Jacob and Elisha and Paul finish their course with the words of the light still on their lips, and the crown of the conqueror still shining on their heads. And the kings that shall arise after them shall be lords even over the Sabbath, or the stopping place of death. "There is no Sabbath keeping in the temple," whispered the rabbis. The Lord of the temple is Lord. He says to the obedient Executive standing still and tall in the flourishing fig tree of fever or dying, "It is finished!" and nothing can resist the Lord's command to the eternally present Obedient God.

The rise of boldness, of authority, is the rise of inborn superiority to surrounding conditions. It is wresting the tongue from outward descriptions to conform to heavenly fact. Authoritative speech brushes aside the cobwebs of outward appearance. It is backed by the mystery of the conquering kingdom of the Inmost Actual.

When Solomon said, "The opening of my lips shall be right things," he meant that he would speak forth from the hidden being of the heart, as free Spirit that knows nothing of defeat or poverty or sickness. By this speech, he would lift his head above conditions. The hidden being of the heart, gifted with dominion, leaps like lightning to expose its magical independence of the length, breadth and thickness of matter, mind, sensations and their world maneuvers.

It is the failure to stand by the things of the Almighty Spirit, which accounts for the seemingly unmanageable misfortunes of aspiring people of all ages. They have supposed, in unguarded moments, that the yielding they must make was to the overbearing three-dimensional effects like misfortune, old age and dying.

Let us heed the voice of inspiration. That yielding which the children of earth are dimly tending to make, is not to the three dimensions but to the God law that works above them. Although now, apparently, by my past downward viewing I have walled myself into feebleness, sickness, defeat, yet, speaking boldly from my bright secret self, I am Strength itself – I am flawless Confidence, I am Master of the willing Good of my universe. This is the "opening of the lips with right things," (Prov. 23:15) and all the divine forces stand ready to minister to my leaping Word.

As the young eagle presses his leathery joints against the cracking shell, all nature waiting in mute sympathy, expecting to be governed by his newborn demands, so the Still God of the universe waits to move through all visible and invisible items to minister in willing docility to my un-diverted high confidence.

"Although the flocks shall be cut off from the fold, and there shall be no herd in the stalls, yet will I joy in the God of my salvation"(Hab 3:17-18) – still forever we hear the voice of the poverty-surrounded Habakkuk singing through the night watches our steadfast example through the ages.

The meekness of the mind, the will and the heart, opening to the Healing Good, is their moving aside for a lordship not of flesh to act. "Watch therefore; for ye know not what hour," (Matt 24:42) your lordship rises.

"As when by drastic lift of pent volcanic fires, the dripping form of a new island springs to meet the airs, so from our deeps we rise."

"Now will I rise, says the Lord, now will I lift up myself" – and "at the lifting up of myself the nations are scattered." (Is 33:10)

It is the rise of the divine will to see, when the blind beggar throws aside his ragged garments and runs to the waiting Jesus. It is the rise of its pent up fragrance when the tightly closed petals of the rose fall back and the hidden splendors of color and perfume face the sun, un-cramped forever.

"Do you ask what Christianity is?" says the sage forgetful of creed and country: "I shall tell it you: It digs up your own ego, and carries it up to God."

It is the rise of the divine ego, which makes us victoriously bold. "Come boldly unto the throne."(Heb 4:16) Boldness has genius, power, and magic in it; what you can dream you can do, begin it. Therefore, be bold! Be persistent!

Though my low views have sent me loss of friends, pain and humiliation, yet truly am I a strong child of God, with dominion in all my vital sap. I am at my roots greater than my environments and the shadows of hardship with which I have darkened my path by turning from the Highest.

Chapter Four – Faith, the Evidence that God is All

Omnipotence stands before me, and behind me, at my right and at my left, above me, and below me, to serve my rising commandings, as He Himself has voiced by priests and prophets, and the young eagle's springing. So we are to look upon the Man who threw aside the wrappings of the grave, the stone-sealed tomb and the soldiers' swords, bursting their three dimensional bindings with risen divinity, as law for all of us, world without end.

Speak in this commanding manner: Let me not turn aside from facing Thee! Deliver Thou me from evil. Thou art empowering Obedience. I owe Thee bold command, O Thou Owner of all the kingdoms!

There is a noble triumvirate of D's on the self-authorizing rock of conquering confidence: David, Daniel and Darius – "Show me a token for good, that they which hate me may see it" – "Let my Lord now speak to me" – "Thy God whom thou servest, He will deliver thee." They show how at the first up-springing of this confidence, this bold certainty, the God in the universe serves promptly. The symbol of this upspring is the emerald stone; stone significant of walking free from common law, unified with the miraculous, where anyone who would hinder us cannot discover us.

This is the science of high visioning – of looking unto the Vast Vast Countenance with healing of our tardy recognition of our own inborn kingship as its fourth gift.

Is not faith the gift of God, according to Scriptural instruction? Is not faith the confidence of things chosen according to the same high information? And does not masterfulness rise with confidence? And are we not told to have the faith, which is the masterfulness of God Himself? "Have the faith of God," said Jesus. (Mk 11:22)

The exaltation of lifting up the vision is "Fear of the Lord." "Pass the time of your sojourning here in fear," (1 Pet 1:17) preached Peter. It is written that the fear of the Lord is the instruction in wisdom. It is written that it is the beginning of wisdom, or light. If your eye seeks the Lord only, your whole body shall be full of wisdom. If your eye seeks the Lord only, He will fulfill your desire. If your eye seeks the Lord only, He will be your strong confidence. If your eye chooses the High Deliverer, your dominion shall rise up.

Thus have the inspired among humanity written in their own risen moments, always showing by their instructions that their risen kingship stirred forth from the bed of lowly-heartedness. And always lowly-heartedness before the Supreme

Chapter Four – Faith, the Evidence that God is All

Majesty, else how should genuine kingship rise with its scepter? "To this man will I look, even to him that trembles at my word," says the Supreme Lord.

Note that Jeremiah prophesied coming greatness and glory while his vision was toward the High and Lofty One that inhabits Eternity, who Himself cannot look upon evil. Seeing sometimes as God sees he sensed the liberation of the Jews from the stream of their forefathers' sins, but never long enough to sense their right to their present Victorious Sonship to their Heavenly Father.

Jesus, the star out of Jacob, bright with the morning of liberation, told them that no man upon the earth was their father. One Only was forever the Father of all, even God. He dipped his speech in the truth of high birth and victorious life. "Neither has this man sinned nor his parents." – "The flesh profits nothing." – "And they shall see His face – And there shall be no night." – "Go ye, and make disciples of all nations."

He taught that those who are steadfast unto the day of believing, commanding confidence and faith shall be saved from the law of cause and effect, the karma of past vision and thought.

According to the law of divine mysticism, the road to learning for the upward watcher is a royal road. Upward watchers know things which they did not know before, and which neither teachers nor books have mentioned. Downward watchers wade through the seas of trouble, and are chided for not having faith. How can they have faith, the substance of things hoped for, when it is the fourth smite from above, reaching down over their own isolated vision to the roots of their own being, and rousing their untaught spark of authority over an un-describable Almighty Executive?

When the spark of faith like a lightning for splendor spoke from the masterful lips of the Unkillable Redeemer, the quickening Mystery back of the tomb and the soldiers' swords flung them all aside, for His free feet to go into Galilee. There the eyes of five hundred saw Him alive and not dead.

Let us write it with a pen of light dipped in the fountain of everlasting truth that we found a new Servant – The Able-to-do all things. "Is there anything too hard for me?"(Gen 18:14) "Before the day was I am He, and there is none that can deliver out of my hand."(Is 43:13) Concerning the works of my hands, command ye me."(Is 45:11) "Kings exercise lordship," said Jesus. How shall anyone be king except his kingship be roused? "By Me kings reign," said the Great Voice that John turned to see. If lions do not stand back, and warrings do not cease, and diseases do not retire,

Chapter Four – Faith, the Evidence that God is All

the true kingship is not among us. Only its crude symbol, working through heavy machinery of army and navy, and jailor and hospital faces us.

Then the disciples asked him to increase their faith. But he answered nothing. For faith, which is kingship exercising to call the God of Lazarus to come forth, and the God of the withered arm to appear, is the deepest secret of all the deep secrets of the *Magia Jesu Christi*.

Seeing then that after speaking with commanding earnestness to Unseeable Majesty, He made insanity and poverty drop their grip, the disciples said, "Lord, teach us to pray."(Lk 11:1) So He taught them to speak firmly and sternly to God, the Great Servant.

He that is greatest among you, let Him be your servant. He that is greatest among us through all eternity is the Lord, Strong and Mighty. None other is greatest.

Your brains do not make your inborn Self greater than the inborn Self of your serf; your money cannot make you greater than the pauper; for God is no respecter of persons, and He surely has made of one blood all the nations. Only One among us is greatest – our Father is He – with name unspeakable on the lips of the downward watcher. His is the kingdom ready to show its finished presence. His is the will to command and the will to obey, identical with the inborn root of obedience and authority inherent in humanity, the highest God and inmost God is one God.

He feeds with super-substantial bread all those who rise up to demand it. He rouses the payment of the debt of confidence to command owing unto Him since ever the world caught us in its wheel. He delivers us at our bold command. He prevents our speech when it chooses the path of disease in description of evil. This is His way and His glory, though you believe it not and take not hold of this key to His kingdom. "He shall feed thee on the Heights of Confidence." (Is 58:14)

The speech of the Lord's Formula being understood as the word of command acts like nutriment to the hidden Jehovah nature. "Man shall feed in the strength of the Lord."(Mic 5:4) It is the end of that feeding on descriptions of goodness or badness, poverty and riches, the pairs of opposites, which Solomon noted as the foolishness that only fools feed upon.

We are taught the obedience of the Good Will fronting us by the golden formula of the Prayer of our Lordship long before we would have formulated it. "I know that his commandment (or the commandment of Him) is life everlasting," said the Messiah. (Jn 12:50) "Thou through the commandments has made me wiser than mine enemies,"(Ps 119:98) cried the glad psalmist. For when I demanded that Thou bow down Thine ear to me, to deliver me speedily, and be my strong rock, then Thy gentleness made me great."

"This is the whole duty of humanity," said Solomon in one of his moments of speaking above his mind, "Fear God, and keep His commandments."

"God manifests His word according to the commandment of God," wrote John the lover. "The commandment of the Lord is pure, enlightening the eyes," wrote one who had touched kingship by watching the high I AM who makes kings. (Ps 19:8)

At the Waters of Lourdes, some patients are taught to repeat the great formula of the hidden Lord in man, called the Lord's Prayer, fifteen times while the curing waters are being tasted.

Has anybody explained to them that the waters of tribulation begin to subside for him who touches the fifteenth cubit above them? Some have caught all their miraculous flashes of genius from much repetition of the seven stately commands of Matthew's Lord's Prayer, or the prayer of our lordship.

Hallowed be Thy name.

Thy kingdom come.

Thy will be done.

Give me this day my super-substantial bread.

Forgive my debt of confidence to command Thee.

Let me not into temptation.

Deliver me from evil.

Who is not glad to utter these words of insistence, that they may be healed of their cringing to old age, death, disease, and poverty?

Chapter Four – Faith, the Evidence that God is All

The fourth Angel being caused to fly swiftly smites all of them of the mystic formula. They are they that keep the commandments of God and the faith of Jesus. The fourth Angel is the bright angel smiting Jacob, smiting Peter, smiting Job "on the left hand where he doth work."

Look unto Him of power to establish according to the mystery which was kept secret since the world began, but now is made manifest according to the commandment of the everlasting God, for the obedience unto faith, as Paul did, writing to the Romans with the pen of that same Victorious Confidence, even to the quickening of the dead Eutychus.

Faith is our *El Shaddai*, our risen recognition of ourselves as Jehovah–Soul. We see the mystery of Divine Obedience everywhere awaiting the kingly rise of our heaven-planted boldness to command, "I will not let Thee go except Thou bless me!"(Gen 32:26) "Thine is the kingdom, and the power, and the glory, forever and ever."(Matt 6:13)

"A Shape looked up from eating herb and grain. It chanced to see the stars, and with that look came wonderment, and longing in its train. The food untasted lay. A beating pain smote at its forehead, but it looked again, and yet again. And then it thought. Lo! Man stood upright as the stars did wane!"

Practice

Bible verses to commit to memory.

- ➢ "Let us therefore come boldly unto the throne of grace."(Heb 4:16)

- ➢ "Faith is the confidence of things hoped for."(Heb 11:1)

- ➢ "In whom we have boldness and access with confidence by the faith of him."(Eph 3:12)

- ➢ "The revelation of the mystery, which was kept secret since the world began, but now is made manifest, according to the commandment of the everlasting God – for the obedience of faith."(Rom 16:25-26)

- ➢ "Concerning the work of my hands command ye me."(Is 45:11)

- "Here are they that keep the commandments of God and the faith of Jesus."(Rev. 14:12)

- "I have overcome the world."(Jn. 16:33)

- "He that hath seen me hath seen the Father."(Jn. 14:9)

- "Let the Lord be thy confidence, he will not suffer thy foot to be taken." (Prov. 3:26)

- "Thou through thy commandments hast made me wiser than mine enemies."(Ps 119:98)

Résumé – Thursday, First Week

That nature, before which we have worshipped, rises up in us. The meek Jesus was worshipper before the King of Kings and Lord of Lords, therefore he must at some moment proclaim, "All power is given unto me in heaven and in earth." (Matt 28:18) "I have overcome the world."(Jn. 16:33) "He that hath seen me hath seen the Father."(Jn. 14:9)

There is no nature worth practicing subservience unto, except the Ruler in the heavens and the earth. "Let the Lord be thy confidence, he will not suffer thy foot to be taken" (Prov. 3:26). "Hast thou faith? Have it to thyself before God."(Rom 14:22)

God is the Author of faith. Jesus of Nazareth caught this so completely that the whole creation was subject to his strong word of authority. Faith is always associated with authority. Faith is confidence to command. One little spark of it, no larger than a mustard seed, would cause authority enough to move a mountain. (Matt 17:20)

Moses caused two million people to obey his lightest command after the spark of authority flamed up in him. He had been meek and lowly to the loss of his self-consciousness, while kneeling before God on the mountains of Midian. Self-consciousness is a poor stuff to present before men or nature if we want to command them even for their good. Is it no self-consciousness that makes a person appear poorly before his neighbors? It is the wiping out of this tough integument that lowliness before the King of Kings accomplishes. Self-consciousness is sometimes called self-will, because it is a perversity of the whole constitution, and because the divine authority that rises out of its demolition is a new will.

Chapter Four – Faith, the Evidence that God is All

Elisha had been lowly before God all his life. He bathed the hands and feet of Elijah while yet his eyes were heavenward. Suddenly, no man in Israel has so much authority over men and nature as the hitherto meek Elisha.

The exercise of authority is a good exercise. It gets its kindling from practicing upon the most obedient servant first. The Supreme God is the most docile and obedient servant. David commanded the High God: "Show me a token for good that they which hate me may see it" (PS 86) He was astonished at the results of his firm authority: "Thou through thy commandments hast made me wiser than my enemies." (PS 119)

Isaiah understood that we must practice commanding the Supreme Presence in the Universe. While listening in lowly humility before Him he heard these words: "Concerning the works of my hands command ye me."(Is 45:11)

Jesus commanded the Supreme Servant, "And now, O Father, glorify thou me with thine own self with the glory which I had with thee before the world was."(Jn 17:5) On the cross he cried, "How Thou hast glorified me!"

Jacob commanded the angel of God's presence, whom he called God himself, "I will not let thee go except thou bless me!"(Gen 82:26) Job said, "I will demand of thee, and declare thou unto me." (Job 42) Jesus commanded the God of Lazarus; He commanded the God of the withered arm. Always lowly meekness rises to confidence to command.

Jesus told his disciples to speak to the Supreme Servant in the terms of the Lord's prayer as the firm insistence of their own lordship or hidden being of the heart whom all authorities obey. It is a formula full of short commands to the Great Servant who asks, "Is anything too hard for me?"(Jer. 82:27)

We will take Thursday to practice speaking to the Great Servant with firm command, in the words of the hidden Lord's Formula. (Matt 6:9-13) We will speak it over and over, fifteen times, as the sick people do at the Waters of Lourdes, when they are urging God to heal them by way of the Waters. Fifteen is the number where the waters of misfortune cease to prevail against us. (Gen 7:20) It is the number of rising to walk above hardship.

Notice that Marcella of the Roman Catholic Church, taught her nuns the inner meaning of "Give us this day our daily bread." She said it ought to be, "Give me this day my super-substantial bread." Our secret ego, our God-spark, our "hidden man of the heart," as Peter called it (I Pet. 3:4), must have the bread of heaven.

Notice how "Lead us not into temptation" has lately been translated as, "Let us not unto temptation," or "Let me not into temptation," meaning, "Warn me when I turn away from Thee." Notice how, "Forgive us our debts," is now understood to be, "Give for our emptiness Thy Substance." Paul's word "substance," is rendered as "confidence," in the margin of Hebrews eleventh chapter, first verse: "Faith is the confidence of things hoped for."

Grow more and more urgent, insistent and commanding, as you go on repeating the Great Formula to the Greatest Servant among us. Let confidence solidify. Let the God-Spark speak.

Chapter Five – Works are the rest of mind in the Presence of God

Friday, First Week

5th Gate - **As spirit, I can preach the gospel, heal the sick, cast out demons, and raise the dead.**

This Lesson is self-active in its treatment power. Do not try to delve into it; make the acknowledgements and let it have its Apostolic way with you.

Prologue

Confidence, or faith in anything, works according to the level of confidence. Conviction is not properly speaking conviction until it develops into action. "Faith without works is dead."(Jas 2:20) Unless some kind of work takes place, we have not believed anything.

Our globe has been called Number Five, the planet of works, since everybody and everything must accomplish something or be nobody and nothing: Sun, Vulcan, Mercury, Venus, Earth. Each to his feat, or opus, till some crowning bloom in earth's garden of humanity cries, "It is finished!"

Earth, as number five, must perform The Great Achievement. The most wonderful achievements of humankind have been brought to pass by confidence in some wonder-working Unseen Power.

Moses and Aaron had a five-pointed star at the end of their mystic wand which they swung high into some unseen perfect land. And when the workings of that land touched this earth they were called miracles: "And Moses stretched forth his rod toward heaven, … and fire ran along upon the ground… and hail smote every herb of the field… only in the land of Goshen where the Children of Israel were, was there no hail… and Moses spread abroad his hands unto the Lord and the thunders and hail ceased" even over all great Pharaoh's land.

All work is redemption. It redeems a place, a people, or a situation from one status into another status.

Chapter Five – Works are the rest of mind in the Presence of God

Redemption is historically associated with the number five. With five loaves did Jesus redeem five thousand people from hunger. With five sling-stones did David redeem all Israel from Goliath the terrible. With five men did Joshua give his people rest from their enemies on the side of Jordan toward the sunrise. With five wounds did Jesus redeem common humankind from ignorance of His Sonship to Royalty Triumphant.

"If a man steal one ox, let him give five oxen for the one ox and he shall be redeemed from the stigma of thief. He shall be restored to his former estate. He shall be reinstated. It shall be as if he had never stolen."

According to John the Revelator, the sardonyx stone, which was the fifth stone of character building, was worn by the ambassador of the King. To him was given power to redeem those who were appointed to destruction. We read that Joseph wore the sardonyx stone as Vice-gerent for Pharaoh, king of Egypt.

It has even been said that Jesus wore the sardonyx stone as ambassador plenipotentiary for the King of Kings and Lord of Lords, but there is no written history for this tradition.

"Five truth mumblings are self active." Five eternal words were said to have been written on the shining garment of Jesus the Glorified.

If we please to look up all that was written about the mystery of Five we shall see how worthy is Number Five to be called The Works Lesson. It answers the Hindu discovery that the best doctrine is that which removes pleasure and grief from the mind; showing that doctrine is self-active. So Fifth, Works, must be a working doctrine, acting on the mind, which affects the body; which body is the working field of mind. Vision affects the mind. Mind is the working field of the vision, as body is the working field of mind.

We always look toward an object before thinking it. Mind glorifies or cramps the body according as the visional sense runs high or low. Nine hundred ninety-nine thousand nine hundred ninety-nine diseases and pains were declared by the Parsees as having been formulated by low visioning acting on mind to afflict its body.

The best ambassador for any king would be a person who would understand the king's mind best and therefore carry out his king's hidden wishes. There is One King of Kings and Lord of Lords, whose whole purpose toward His kingdom has ever been

Chapter Five – Works are the rest of mind in the Presence of God

peace, health, wisdom, and majesty even to the greatness and wisdom of His Own Self: "Look unto Me."(Is 45:22) "I extend peace like a river."(Is 66:12) "I am the Lord that heals thee."(Ex 15:26) "I will instruct thee and teach thee."(Ps 32:8) These are the words of the High Redeemer inhabiting Eternity, whose way upon the earth is the saving health of the nations.

The Ambassador Plenipotentiary for this High Redeemer said that the same fountain cannot send forth both bitter and sweet. So when we have pain or poverty or sickness or misfortune of any kind we must have been looking away from the High Redeemer, who counsels: "Seek ye My face and live."(Amos 5:4)

Let us not be deceived by the poetic eloquence of any great poet or theologian who tells us that The King of Kings suffers or is in anyway grieved. For if He suffers or is grieved, He must shed suffering and grief around Him, even as we when suffering and grieved shed suffering and grief in all directions.

Those who speak of the King of Kings reporting that He is angry with the wicked every day, or that anything grieves or dismays Him, are not ambassadors understanding the Great King's mind. They are ambassadors for their own kind of king, and their own kind of king works his own way with them.

There are some wounds on life's pathway that only the Real Christ Jesus can heal.

Read the words of Zoroaster of Persia eighteen hundred years before the coming of the Anointed of the Heavenly King: "A virgin shall conceive and bear a son, and a star shall appear at midday to signalize the occurrence. When you behold the star, follow it wherever it leads you. Adore the mysterious Child, offering Him gifts with profound humility. He is indeed the Almighty Word. He is indeed your Lord and everlasting King."

There is a science, which runs like a river of light above all the sciences. It never changes its assurances. It tells of the Working Efficiency of One Lord Supreme and how the language runs that describes the Working Efficiency.

It is the Mystical Science. According to its practice we never say we fight for the Lord Supreme, but "The Lord shall fight for us and we shall hold our peace." (Ex 14:14) We never say we trust a friend, but "All my trust on Thee is stayed."(Ps 7:1, 16:1)

Chapter Five – Works are the rest of mind in the Presence of God

"Put not your trust in princes," (Ps 146:3) is the language of the Lord Supreme; "I will contend with him that contends with you."(Is 49:25) "No man shall set on you to hurt you."(Acts 18:10) "Fear not, I will help you."(Is 41:10) "Look unto Me."(Is 45:22)

Mystical Science starts the New Language promised to break forth from the lips of humankind at some time: "I will turn to the people a pure language."(Zeph. 3:9) "They shall speak with new tongues."(Mk 16:17)

Whatever language humanity starts up with, shows that visional sense has preceded speech. For "I have made you like unto Him, even God who calls those things which be not as though they were."

He can throw his vision out toward damage for some neighbor and silently mentioning the damage in definite terms he will find it formulated in the experience of that neighbor. But "Add to your strength, knowledge," said Peter. Is it not written that the one who imagined the damage of his neighbor, fell and injured the very limb he had imagined himself using with neighbor-damaging violence? Can you see how much we need the high watch with its high language? People must learn the law of lifting up their faces to the Lord Supreme who brings noble conditions of life into view.

How shall we make it plain that power, and vigor, and plenty, hail from above, with no need to maltreat or suborn our neighbor?

Things and people are often troublesome. Mystical Science teaches us to let them alone as if they did not exist. To look up to the Vast Vast Countenance for one second of time; maybe two seconds; to have nothing to do with them; to cut the threads of attention toward them. The Vast Vast Countenance says: "I will set them in order before your eyes," (Ps 50:21) "I restore to you the years that the locust hath eaten." (Joel 2:25)

Have not locusts always been symbolic of domestic tormenting? Restorations hail from above. Expect greatly from above, and greatly shall restorations multiply. "Prove me now herewith, says the Lord of hosts, if I will not pour you out a blessing that there shall not be room enough to receive it."(Mal 3:10)

So it is that Self-recognition awakens. So is new mind built. So is hidden ability set astir. So arises the new race of which Jesus was the forerunner.

Chapter Five – Works are the rest of mind in the Presence of God

No man has ever stood so boldly forth for the Redemption of the God-Self of humanity from the clutches of the mortality-self, as that young man of despised old Nazareth two thousand years ago! No lover of his brothers and sisters so willing to die has ever appeared on this earth so that He might show us our own God transcendence. He knew the ancient doctrine preached in many ways that humanity was the offspring of satan with only one God glow in their being, and that the angels dwelling in glorious Paradise had asked each other who was willing to leave his heavenly home to redeem the God of man from the satan of man and daringly declare to humanity: "For this cause came I forth into the world."(Jn. 18:37)

> Why should not now the angels,
> On heights of untold glory,
> Sing often time the story
> Of the greatest one among them,
> Christ Jesus and His Love...

Works

It was practicing inborn authority over the Universal Servitor, when the wonderful Jesus cried, "Glorify Thou Me!" (Jn 17:5) and when on the cross He acknowledged, "How Thou hast glorified Me," (Jn 17:4) He was seeing the obedience of the obedient God to His orders. His eye overlooked future ages, when He should stand to humankind as the embodiment of divine insistence - His Name above principalities and powers, and above every name that could be named.

Abraham was practicing inborn authority over the Invisible Servitor, when he said, "I lift up mine hand unto the Lord, the most high God, the possessor of heaven and earth. – Whereby shall I know that I inherit the land? Show me a sign." And he was experiencing the obedience of God when a deep sleep fell upon him, and he saw himself famed for spiritual and material riches throughout all succeeding generations.

David was practicing innate authority over the Universal Obedience, when he said, "Be Thou my strong rock! Deliver me speedily!" And when David's little band of warriors had swelled into "a great host, like the host of God," and he had been three times crowned king, he was in the thick of God's obedience.

Gideon was practicing the same inborn authority, when he spoke to the Universal Servitor, "Show me a sign that Thou talkest with me." And when fires rose up out of a rock, and the Midianites and Amalekites and all the children of the East fell down at the sight of Gideon, then the Great Servant was obeying Gideon's bold prayer of lordship.

Chapter Five – Works are the rest of mind in the Presence of God

Authority with the Universal Servant is roused in us to accomplishing vigor, by repeating the prayer of our inborn lordship, with firmness and sternness.

Authority with the universally present Divine Servant discloses authority with the particularly present divine Self, or Spirit of God vivifying each frame. "He that rules his own spirit is better than he that takes a city."(Prov. 16:32)

Someone addressed his own body whenever it fell into weakness, seeing it as charged with the intelligent and individually present Godship, "Rise up strong and active; be competent to do all my work this day; throw aside pain!" It was the God charging every molecule and atom of him with competent obedience that slowly stirred from its quiescence into energetic activity, intelligently obeying his orders, making him strong and healthy for the day.

The self of self-subdued humanity is as the Supreme Self, or God. The Eternal Immanence is in the present tense exactly as in the past, and the still intelligence that waits at every infinitesimal pore of our human frame, today, as yesterday, leaps into action if we command with firmness and sweet sternness. So now let us according to orders, "Up-raise the self by the divine Self; for the divine Self is the friend of self."

Every night before the eyes close in slumber we should command the immanent Godship swelling the self with possibilities to do the work we choose to accomplish, also what type of character we choose to exhibit. "Awake up, my glory!" (Ps 57:8) commanded David and his glory awoke. "Shake thyself from the dust; arise, and sit down, O Jerusalem; loose thyself from the bands of thy neck, O captive daughter of Zion!"(Is 52:2) shouted Isaiah to himself. And Isaiah transcended all the prophets that have ever lived on earth; he was loosed from all dependence on the instructions of humankind.

The divine Self of our self has a voice. Its answer to every command we give it, "I can do all that and more." Why should we fall asleep regretting the day or dreading the morrow, when we have an eternally abiding divine Self, quiescent, still, instinct with executiveness, waiting our firm insistence on Its action in our behalf?

We must be up and about the business of managing our own God-ness in us, and command the vitality of our own mind to remember all things, and the vigor of our own hearts to beat with steady hardihood. And so our mind will remember all things, even its relation to Universal Spirit that raises the dead. It is said that Apollinius, a Greek philosopher, realized this and his heart beat so in rhythm with the universal possibilities of himself that he was able to be in two places at once, whenever necessary.

"The upright shall have dominion," (Ps 49:14) chanted the Hebrew choirs under the leadership of David.

Praise is comely for the upright, for the "I" the Soul-Self, the God-Self is one with praise as with command, ready to demonstrate all excellence for which It is praised, all accomplishments to which It is commanded. The voice of inspiration teaches us to praise Soul, the upright Self charging ourself like a Shekinah pillar of fire by night, and a straight cloud of glory by day.

Let us not speak without praise for our "I" our secret free Spirit, saying, "I am sick," or, "I am discouraged," or "I am inconsequent" – for this is speaking out of key with high truth. "I was free born," said Paul, speaking in key with truth. We were all free born, upheld by Free Spirit forever. By recognizing this we bring It to the front. Truth is mighty in itself, and whoever fights for high truth has forgotten its almightiness. Paul represents those of us sensing our free estate by simple recognition of our free Divinity.

"Lo, my sheaf stood upright," praised Joseph, visioning ahead when the Jews of all ages should owe their daily bread to his fidelity to praise of his own divine Self, maintaining his own vision of himself, even while in prison, as one instinct with majesty and virile with omnipotence. He once had his ordinary senses entranced as in a dream, while his sense of God-ness rose like an incense, and remembering this, he told his fellow prisoners the import of their dreams, while yet his own dream was unfulfilled. He knew that truth is truth whether we are already embodiments of it or not.

Poets by setting their words and thoughts into tune with the soundless whispers of their own laws of Soul life, have often struck the chords of Self praise like wonderful antiphons:

> "Thou shalt flourish in immortal youth,
> Unhurt amid the war of elements,
> The wreck of matter and the crush of worlds."

> "Wingless upon your pinions forth I fly,
> My words begin to breathe upon your breath:
> Shorten half way my road to heaven from earth."

Chapter Five – Works are the rest of mind in the Presence of God

> "It were a vain endeavor, though I should gaze forever
> At that green light that lingers in the west;
> I may not hope from outward forms to win
> The passion and the life whose fountains are within."

The muscles of the body can be trained to be so strong that they can beat down giants in gymnasiums and pugilistic encounters. Thoughts of the mind can be trained to be so strong that they can strike down opposing ideas on invisible mind fields, and paralyze the judgments of the brain so that judges and juries speak nothing, or, speaking, speak only nonsense. Muscles highly trained have won out against natural muscles, and thoughts highly practiced have wrought mental havoc.

What shall we, who wish to be free and not to engage in warfare do, when our peace and safety are menaced by foes of such giant physical and mental stature? We will seek unto God, the high presence in the universe not affected by thoughts: we will seek unto Him present at our own headquarters, Whose years alter not, Who says, "These all shall perish but I, Soul, Self, shall endure."(Ps 102:26) "Seek ye Me, and ye shall live."(Amos 5:4) "No weapon formed against thee shall prosper." (Is 54:17)

It shall not profit us to gain the whole world by the prowess of our arm or the might of our thought. It shall only profit us to know our own Soul, uncontaminated offspring of Eternal Majesty, whose triumphs are already complete, ready to manifest. "The Highest God and inmost God is One God."

Let mind no longer claim creative powers or accomplishing energies. The true work is already complete in Spirit, the Self that we praise. "I am all that and more," answers Soul, our own "I," to our highest descriptions. "I can all that and more," It answers to our highest mandates.

Soul has strength of empire and an influential glory such as it has not entered into the heart of humanity to conceive.

Our own Soul, our own free Spirit forever says, in bold faith, "I am Truth, I am God --- Omnipresence, Omnipotence, and Omniscience."

The outer appearance, the cocoon, the hard chrysalis, vibrates when the words of Immortal Soul are spoken silently or audibly, as the chandelier hums when its key-note is struck, or as the brim of a bell resounds when its hidden tongue hits it.

Chapter Five – Works are the rest of mind in the Presence of God

Paganini said that he could shake any building by maintaining the note that caused it to vibrate. By speaking the truth of and to our own Soul, or Self, we strike the true key tone to the body of flesh and its mind and emotions. We can speak in silent language or audible words the truth of the transcendental Self that causes health, happiness, and helpfulness to radiate; and this speech wakes the Soul type of humanity to walk on earth.

A great modern philosopher says, "The Spirit is ever rising up in wrath against the forces that would brutalize it; the Soul is ever striving for independence of matter." But the truth of Soul is that it ever dwells in calm majesty, striving against nothing. Nothing can injure the immortal principle of the soul. "Truly my soul waits upon God," (Ps 62:1) sang David to a noble tune on a stringed instrument – "Truly my soul waits on God." And the angry javelin of the angry Saul could not reach him, for he had keyed himself to uninjurable Immortal Soul, by voicing Its invigorating truth.

It is not what happens to us that makes us healthy, happy, and radiantly helpful; it is what we harmonize with, and we harmonize with what we describe. The winds of misfortune and pain hit every one, sooner or later; but they do not touch our Self. "Truly my soul waits upon God," we sing. (Ps 62:1) "My soul does magnify the Lord," we chant. (Lk. 1:46)

We set ourselves to the heavenly Soul key by praising our innate Lordship, our eternal identification with Divinity. "It is the set of the soul that decides the goal, and not the storms of life."

We praise the great free Spirit that stands back of our mind. We praise the free Spirit that knows beyond the mind, which is always saying, "I am God - I am Truth - I am Light" – and so we touch the law of the "five." For when the fifth angel sounds, the sun and air are darkened to the vision of John the Revelator. He means, that by recognizing our divine, "I," our mind ceases to be our supreme guide, and the sensations are forgotten.

There is a consciousness of cold, there is a consciousness of heat, there is a consciousness of stinging, and of falling or rising; so there is a consciousness of God. It is consciousness as in a trance; and John calls it the darkening of the sun and the air; for John is always speaking in figures.

Those who have the consciousness of God know beyond their minds, and wake a new kind of body, in tune with the Infinite Immortal, the Lord Supreme.

Chapter Five – Works are the rest of mind in the Presence of God

Praise and command of the divine Self of our self, always wakes the consciousness of our own superiority to environing disadvantages and ignorance. "Know Thyself" was written over the Delphic Temple.

It is only the divine Self, Soul, free Spirit that is worth knowing, worth praising, worth commanding.

Fight as though you were the fighter, but know that it is but the free spirit of you that moves on the opposing phalanxes that try to make life difficult – and the free Spirit masters them though the mind and the flesh quake. Jacob trembled all night by the Jabbok brook, and his mind was afraid, but the Angel of God's presence, with whom he had identified himself, fought his battle for him, "I have seen God face to face," he said "and my life is preserved."(Gen 32:30) "The Angel which redeemed me from all evil, bless the lands."(Gen 48:16)

In the Fourth Study we are taught to practice the prayer of our lordship. John the Revelator calls this the smoke of the incense arising from the pit of our own infinite possibilities, for the highest and the inmost are one in infinitude. "And the smoke of the incense, which came with the prayers of the saints, ascended up before God out of the angel's hand." And one came like a star from the skies, showing to all humanity their own infinite possibilities, through recognizing the identity of the Soul of each person with the majesty of Almighty God. The infinite possibilities of Soul, our God Self, are spoken of in the Apocalypse as "the bottomless pit."

When Naomi recognized Ruth as her leader and guide, and the light of her life, she was recognizing Spirit, and forgetting her unhappy mind and emotions. "Entreat me not to leave thee," said Ruth "nor from following after thee, for where thou goest I will go." And Naomi, by her acceptance of Ruth, became forebear of Christ the Savior. So our Soul, our Ruth, is ever saying to us, "Where thou goest, I will go," (Rut 1:16) through the ages – always waiting in quiescence, in shining esse, for acknowledgment by praise and command.

Our secret Self ever whispers: "You cannot praise Me so highly that I am not more than you praise, You cannot command Me so greatly that I cannot work by you still more greatly."

The young Jesus stood up in old Nazareth and spoke of the everlasting Son of God, the Immortal Youth, the Unconquerable Divinity of humanity, and the Nazarenes tried to throw Him off a precipice, to destroy Him and His words. They refused to recognize their own divinity, their self-renewing fountain of immortality.

Chapter Five – Works are the rest of mind in the Presence of God

So old Naomi, accepting what Nazareth rejected, was prophecy that the seed of the woman should bruise the serpent's head – or, that the vision of woman toward the ever fresh fountain of divinity should save the world from the hard rulership of mind and matter.

When the mind no longer conceives itself to be the knower, recognizing that Free Spirit is the Knower and the Doer, only then can humanity be liberated from the laws of mind and matter.

It was by the recognition of His own Infinite Divinity, His own God-ness, that Jesus of Nazareth discovered His ability to perform the greatest work ever accomplished upon this earth, and made Himself the Bloom in the Garden of Man.

It is through divine at–one-ment that He accomplished his great helpfulness to the world. He saw Himself as the fulfillment of the prophecies of the ages that one should come who should be greater than death, pain, and grief and all the hatred of the entire human race. He saw Himself so identified in the flesh with flawless, unhurtable Substance that He could take to Himself all the pains and the discords of the human race, and yet not be slain, and yet be nothing less than Divinity.

He saw that whoever should acknowledge His accomplishment in future ages should be set free from their own pains and discords. They then should sense that Jesus of Nazareth, charged with His own divinity, was the Savior of the world from disease and death, misfortune and decay, even here and now upon this earth, in the sight of all humanity. "Who gave himself for us," said Paul, "that he might deliver us from this present evil world."(Gal 1:4)

"Who hath believed our report, and to whom is the arm of the Lord revealed?" wrote Isaiah, (Is 53:1) visioning ahead when the Savior of the world, as the arm of the Lord revealed, should not be acknowledged as having destroyed death by taking into His own body the sum total of death, and not acknowledged as having destroyed disease and pain by having taken into His Divinity-charged body the sum total of disease and pain, that all humanity might go free by the acknowledgment. Yet, "Surely He hath borne our griefs and carried our sorrows" (Is 53:4) that we might go free from grief and sorrow. "Surely He was wounded for our transgressions, He was bruised for our iniquities; the chastisement of our peace was upon Him; and with His stripes we are healed." (Is 53:5)

When Jesus, the Bloom in the Garden of Man, came and charged Himself completely with the Divine Presence in the universe, He fulfilled the prophecy of the

Jews that one should come who should be so at one with Absolute God, that He could be slain and yet not dead, diseased and yet immaculate, who should chemicalize out of existence, and thus make nothing, all the maladies of earth. The condition of others being consciously and visibly saved by this exercise of His divinity should forever be, the acknowledgment of this accomplishment.

"When thou shalt make His soul an offering for sin … the pleasure of the Lord shall prosper in His hand." (Is 53:10) What is the pleasure of the Lord? "It is your Father's good pleasure to give you the kingdom." (Lk 12:32)

Jesus of Nazareth had His work, as we each of us have a work, which is supremely ours, and no other can accomplish this opus, or God-ordained work save our own self. The work of Jesus was the redemption of humankind from sin, sickness, and death, by the withdrawal into Himself, by virtue of His supernal God-ness, all the sin, sickness and death of the universe, leaving the universe entirely without sin, sickness and death, thus allowing us to walk through a redeemed world.

This was His chosen work, and it is only fair to Him, Jesus of Nazareth, charged to the supreme with Christ power, that humanity should acknowledge the completeness and splendor of His finished chosen work.

The inspired Scriptures are explicit on the subject of His successfully accomplishing in the large, what Elisha and Elijah accomplished in the small, in the way of taking death into Himself, that He might deliver them who through the expectation of death were subject to its bondage all their lifetime, destroying him that hath the power of death, that is, the devil, the lie from the beginning, abolishing death once and for all. "Who hath saved us, and called us with a holy calling, not according to our works – who hath abolished death." (2 Tim 1:9)

It is a well-known observation that certain people by putting themselves into the consciousness of God can withdraw sickness, pain, disease, deformity and death into themselves, leaving the sufferer free from his sufferings. This vicarious suffering is often taken in our own day, by sensitive and spiritually illuminated men and women, who are not awake enough to chemicalize the condition into nothingness. This is why we often wonder why spiritually sensitive and divinely illuminated people are sometimes afflicted in mysterious ways.

Only Jesus of Nazareth understood how to withdraw the wretchedness of the people into Himself consciously. He made wretchedness nothing both for them and

Chapter Five – Works are the rest of mind in the Presence of God

for Himself. He did it by the consciousness of His own God Substance, His own majestic, untarnishable Soul.

Isaiah, the prophet, gave the assurance that all should go free from their own sorrows and sicknesses, who should acknowledge that Jesus of Nazareth, by the Soul or the Christ splendor shining through Him, had borne their griefs and carried their sorrows, taken their infirmities and borne their sicknesses.

Mistakes of mind and action may be conscious or unconscious. When mistakes are unconscious people may never trace the mechanical consequences of their mistakes to the misfortunes of daily life.

This is where the offer of Jesus the Christ, vicarious bearer of all the sufferings and all the unwitting causes of sufferings for the whole world -- the destroyer of karmic death and disease, should be acknowledged. This acknowledgment is the same as passing on all distress to the Healing Fountain: "Himself took our infirmities and bare our sicknesses," and "redeemed us from the curse of the law."(Matt 8:17)

There is no describing what worldwide liberation from suffering might be manifested, by making "His Soul the offering for sin" (Eph 5:1) and its consequences, since the sacred promise remains on eternal pages, that, "God the Father gives us the spirit of wisdom and revelation, for the acknowledgment of Him," which acknowledgment the world has not yet made. (Eph 1:17)

Peter and Paul among the early Apostles of the Christian doctrine were the most definite and distinct in proclamations concerning the mysterious mission of the Lord Jesus of Nazareth.

Paul wrote to the Galatians, "God sent forth his Son, made of a woman, made under the law, to redeem them that were under the law."(Gal 4:4-5) "Christ has redeemed us from the curse of the law, being made a curse for us." (Gal 3:13)

To the Corinthians, Paul wrote that "God was in Christ, reconciling the world unto himself, not imputing their trespasses unto them." (2 Cor 5:19) And to Titus, he wrote "Who gave himself for us, that he might redeem us from all iniquity."(Tit 2:14)

In calling the attention of the Hebrew Christians to the majesty of the fulfillment of the law in the history of the Redeemer, he said, "We are sanctified through the offering of the body of Jesus Christ once for all."(Heb 10:10) "How shall we escape if we neglect so great a salvation?"(Heb 2:3)

Paul further explained that Jesus had given Himself for us all that He might redeem us from all iniquity.

It was reiterating the insistence of Jesus Himself that the "Son of Man came to give His life a ransom for many," (Mat 20:28, Mk 10:45)when Paul wrote so boldly of Him "who gave Himself for our sins, that He might deliver us from this present evil world," (Gal 1:4) "Who though He was rich, yet for our sakes He became poor, that we through His poverty might be rich." (2 Cor 8:9)

Paul does not try to argue us into the acceptance of the principles of vicarious suffering, and the liberation from suffering, accomplished by acknowledging who hath suffered vicariously, for Paul was a Jew of the strictest sect of the Pharisees, and to him it was the natural religion that one should be made a sufferer for the transgressions of many.

Paul had been brought up on the belief that the transgressions of many might, even as a religious sacrament, be solemnly passed on to some innocent animal in the wilderness.

He wrote to the hard headed and heavily diseased Corinthians, "For the preaching of the cross is to them that perish, foolishness, but unto us which are saved, it is the power of God."(I Cor 1:18)

Peter's words are vivid and emphatic like Paul's: "Who His own Self bare our sins, in His own body on the tree, that we, being dead to sin, should live unto righteousness, by whose stripes we are healed," (1 Pet 2:24) for "Christ has suffered for us in the flesh," and "once suffered for sins, that He might bring us to God." (1 Pet 3:18)

We are all posited on this planet for the one purpose of accomplishing some great opus, or work of a unique and inimitable sort. We do this by the recognition of our own divinity, our own free bold spirit, offspring of Almighty Jehovah. We have the example among the multitudinous sons of men, of One who was the first fruits of them that slept in non-recognition of their own divine equipment.

"For now is Christ risen from the dead, that both He that sanctifies and he that is sanctified might be one."

There is no respect of persons with God. Though Jesus of Nazareth was indeed the first to accomplish the superhuman, by the recognition of His own superhuman equipment, there is no reason why each one of us should not rise up and accomplish the super-mission which we came here to accomplish for the glory of our Eternal Father.

This is the great planet of achievement. Every individual upon it naturally seeks to accomplish some beautiful and praise-worthy deed.

We must remember and acknowledge that only One of us has really accomplished His native deed of unspeakable splendor by full recognition of His own unspeakable, splendid Divinity.

As it has taken the light of some splendid stars thousands of years to reach our earth, so it has taken the best part of two thousand years for humankind to recognize the far-reaching glory of the undertaking of the Divinity-charged Jesus of Nazareth.

Christ Jesus as Emmanuel, or God with us, has once borne my mistaken actions and their consequences for me, that I might be unloaded of my life blunders and be free to accomplish my own great task.

Christ Jesus as Emmanuel, or God with us, has once taken to Himself the mistaken thoughts of my mind and their consequences that I might be unveiled of my mind, and free with my bold Soul, my uncovered free Spirit, to speak new words of victorious truth.

Christ Jesus as Emmanuel, or God with us, has once borne for me the burdens of my human lot, that I might be unburdened free Spirit forever. "He is the propitiation for my sins, and not for mine only, but for the sins of the whole world."(I Jn. 2:2) That it might be fulfilled which was spoken of by Isaiah the prophet saying, "Himself took our infirmities and bare our sicknesses ... Bore our griefs and carried our sorrows, that we might not bear them." (Is 53:4)

All the learnedness of the world cannot compass the wonder of the mind of Christ, who knew all things and needed not that any man should teach Him. The highest point of His wisdom was His understanding of how to be God, glowing and transfiguring through the flesh, even to the annulment of all its mortal liability; and how to transfigure the mind with new light, so that no more errors could darken it.

Jesus knew how to be so mighty with Omnipotence that all who should recognize Him should share His mightiness. Whoever confesses that Christ has actually once come through the flesh, partakes of the coming, and are themselves sent as workers of new work, and speakers of new words.

Who is ready, by acknowledgment, to wash sometimes in this pool of Siloam, or complete negation of himself, in heavenly abandon to the great Scripturally proclaimed Neutral to the sin of the world, living only as "Christ that lives in me?"

This is becoming dead with Christ that we may live with Him, "For if we be dead with Christ, we shall also live with Him." (Rom 6:8) Jesus was truly unified with highest God only, as positive magnet is unified with negative magnet only, so only the God of man could gather to Him to abide, and only the Christ can gather to all who let themselves go with Him in full acknowledgment of His having put all things under His feet, tasting death once for every man, suffering, the just for the unjust, as Master of all things.

"Turn ye even to Me with fasting, and behold, I will send you corn and wine and oil. Fear not, O land, for I will do great things." (Joe 2)

It makes a great difference to us what doctrine we mine out of the Scriptures, and the Apostolic Christians surely mined from them, the doctrine that Jesus blotted out the handwriting of ordinances against us, taking it out of the way, nailing it to His cross.

Abraham was the pivotal man of sustained faith in individual good due from the Universal Absolute. Jesus was the pivotal man of achievement of the humanly impossible by the identification of himself with the divinely possible.

The Chaldeans had prophesied of Him as the Lofty One to arrive among humankind. The Egyptians had foreseen Him as the Lord of the whole world to come among us. The Chinese had waited for Him as the Saving One, who would be born, and would die for the race. The Hebrews had expected Him as darkness expects light.

It is ours to let ourselves bathe in the Siloam waters of yielding, under Scriptural orders, as meekly as the blind man bathed in Siloam of old, declaring the Scripture doctrine of Christ Jesus as the first Divinity-awakened laborer in the vineyard, redeeming the world from sin, sickness, and death, that we might perceive with open eyes that we are walking through a finished kingdom, the arm of the Lord revealed. This is fasting from our sense of obligation to heal the sick, cast out demonic tempers, and raise the dead, since in Christ Jesus these works are finished, awaiting only acknowledgment to be plainly visible.

"Is it not this fast that I have chosen," said the Lord "to loose the bands of wickedness, to undo the heavy burdens, to let the oppressed go free, and take off every yoke?" (Is 58:6)

Let us go daringly free into Scriptural declarations, as this is pure Scriptural doctrine of vicarious bearing, mentioned distinctly to an age lost to all belief in the truth of the cross, though "all the light of the sacred story gathers round its head sublime."

Great signs shall follow them that believe in the Redemptive labor of the Divinity-awakened Lord of Galilee. They shall disclose the heavenly health of the redeemed world their opened eyes perceive – the world free from sin, sickness, death, misfortune, and mourning. "For there is a kingdom on this earth, though not of it, that is a fact, as our hearts are facts, and we journey through this kingdom from birth to death without seeing it; nor shall any man see it till he first knows his own Soul."

Jesus of Nazareth, the Deific Man, is leading the generations into a new age, into new works where they may shine forth, through sighting with mystically opened eyes the Kingdom of Love and Life immortal and uncontaminate that lies all about them.

"When thou shall make His Soul the offering - the pleasure of the Lord shall prosper."(Is 53:10) "For it is your Father's good pleasure to give you the kingdom."(Lk 12:32)

Practice

Bible verses to commit to memory:

> - "And the word was made flesh, and dwelt among us, and we beheld his glory, the glory as of the only begotten of the father full of grace and truth."(Jn 1:14)

> - "Behold, my sheaf stood upright."(Gen 37:7)

Chapter Five – Works are the rest of mind in the Presence of God

- ➢ "He that ruleth his spirit is better than he that taketh a city." (Prov 16:32)

- ➢ "Pleasant words are sweet to the soul."(Prov 16:24)

- ➢ "When thou shalt make his soul an offering."(Is 53:10)

- ➢ "I have finished the work Thou gavest me to do."(Jn 17:4)

- ➢ "As far as the east is from the west, so far hath he removed our transgressions from us."(Ps 103:12)

- ➢ "That he might deliver us from this present evil world."(Gal 1:4)

- ➢ "Awake up, my glory!"(Ps 57:8)

- ➢ "Awake thou that sleepest!"(Eph 5:14)

- ➢ "God sent forth his son to redeem them that were under the law." (Gal 4:5)

Résumé - Friday First Week

Faith without works does not exist. Faith always works. It stirs boldness and confidence, to dare the seemingly impossible. Notice Elisha's bold faith when he ordered the widow to borrow vessels and pour oil, seemingly from nowhere, into them. (2 Kings 4)

Command of the Great Servant is a practice that changes the nature from timidity and doubt to commanding boldness. It changes the nature from timid following to daring leadership and from obedience to authority. So was Jacob's name changed to Israel, when he fought with the angel at daybreak, and won in the battle. (Gen 32)

Authority with God discloses authority with the Self. The divine Self lies quiescent and still, waiting in all humankind to be stirred into action by the outer self. Two kinds of action stir the still Self into action: command and praise.

Once the Spirit is recognized, it acts. Recognition has a subtle law of its own. Body and its speech are woven into relationship with the Soul, or Self, by recognition.

Chapter Five – Works are the rest of mind in the Presence of God

We are to turn and speak to the divine Self back of us. As our speech has so far been shot forward, speaking to our neighbor, so now at the turn of the tongue, we speak backward to raise up our outer self by our hidden Self. This Self back of us, like a *Shekinah* pillar of cloud by day and of fire by night, is the friend of our outer self or outer life. It can make the outer life whole, strong, and sane. For the truly sane know, that health can be awakened outwardly by the recognition of the Soul's free, flawless and immortal excellence. "The Spirit of a man is the candle of the Lord."(Ps 20:27) And by recognizing this candle sound health is established in the outer experience. "Awake up, my glory!"(Ps 57:8) "Awake thou that sleepest!"(Eph 5:14) This is addressing with ever-strong command the ever-present, glorious Soul.

Those whose Soul glows and flames through all they do and think, have discovered a bottomless well of living refreshment to draw from. Everything they do has the touch of spiritual charm about it. For the Soul is the everlasting reservoir of enchantment. "The fifth angel sounded," said John the Revelator (Rev 9:1) and a star-like character appeared upon the depths of their own Soul, or the bottomless well of power and glory. And John saw that the being of Soul showed humankind how to put their consciousness of flesh limitation and common sensation of pain and pleasure into trance, or sleep, for the sense of God's Presence to be most real. And thereby humanity should know new laws of life.

For centuries, we have been urged to praise and command the hidden limitless divine Self of us. Let us begin now, to praise and command the divine Self: "Oh Wonderful Me! Oh, strong and unspoilable Me! Beautiful Me! Influential Me! Enchanting and Immortal Wisdom!" It answers, "I am all that, and more." For "Eye hath not seen, nor ear heard, neither have entered into the heart of man, the things which God hath prepared for them that love him. But God hath revealed them unto us by his Spirit: for the Spirit searcheth all things, yea, the deep things of God."(I Cor 2:9-10)

Let us continue with strong commands to our great Self: "Rise up, my Soul, and heal the sick wherever I walk! Show people how to be strong! Make people love God! Quicken me with heavenly fervor! Show me the finished kingdom through which I walk! Show me the words that make the world glad and sane!" The Soul, or Free Spirit, answers: "I can all that and more."

We must never give over commanding the Soul Self, every night before we sleep. Some day, like Jesus of Nazareth, we shall sense our ever-present abilities. It was by the sense of his masterful Soul that Jesus saw he could take all the sin and all the consequences of the sins of the world into himself. Because he was full of the Godhead bodily, he could utterly annihilate sin, sickness, and death.

There is a strange and very little observed law ever operating among us. It is the law of vicarious or transferred suffering. Jesus saw this law and entered it, and for all who would accept his great offer, there is freedom from unconscious or mechanical guilt. Jesus offered to take our guilt and the consequences of guilt into his own self, and thereby lift the weight of the law. "God sent forth his son to redeem them that were under the law."(Gal 4:5) He offered to do this for all unwitting sinners upon the earth. "He is the propitiation for our sins, and not for ours only, but also for the sins of the whole world."(I Jn 2:2)

Let us acknowledge the great, unprecedented, and uncopiable achievement of Jesus of Nazareth, who, by recognition of his own Soul, did the humanly impossible. He is the pivotal man. He is the Soul-bloom in the garden of man, the first fruits of them that slept. (I Cor 15:20)

We will take Friday to acknowledge before High God the surpassing accomplishment of Jesus of Nazareth. Let us acknowledge before God, that we walk through a redeemed, healed, unpunishable world, because of the vicarious suffering of Jesus of Nazareth. He, being all God-hood, was and is forever Christ Jesus – or God Jesus – the living manifestation of what humanity can do and be by recognition of their own son-ship to Omnipotence. "That God the Father may give you the spirit of Wisdom and revelation for the acknowledgment of him."(Eph 1:17)

Let us accept our liberty. Let us accept our health; let us accept our redemption, by stating what hath been done. So shall we by sighting one completed work enter upon our own ordained opus. "God is not unrighteous that he will forget our work."(Heb 6:10)

There is but one unit one, but as many expressions of the unit one as we please. Each expression occupying an independent and differentiated position, so there is but One Supreme Self in the universe. It manifests as the Self of Jesus, or your-self, or my-self. There is but one work for each of us. As Jesus did his work, so we are to do ours.

Every Friday, let us lift up our voices to acknowledge that, "Jesus Christ, as Emmanuel, God with us, hath borne my griefs and carried my sorrows. He was wounded for my transgressions. He was bruised for my iniquities, the chastisement of my peace was upon him, and by his stripes I am healed. He Himself took my infirmities and bore my sicknesses. He is the propitiation for my sins and not for mine only but for the sins of the world."(Is 53:4 -5) This acknowledgment is promised to send ether balm across the heart and brain.

As Divine Mind, which I am, I can preach the Gospel, I can heal the sick, I can cast out demons, I can raise the dead. I work the works of God, who works through me to will and to do that which ought to be done by me. I do this according to the doctrine of Jesus Christ: "The words that I speak unto you, I speak not of myself, but the Father that dwelleth in me, he doeth the works." (Jn 14:10)

Thus the highest working power is to see that we have nothing to do – the Spiritual world is already perfect.

Chapter Six - Understanding of God

Saturday & Sunday, First Week

6th Gate - **I understand the secret of instantaneous spiritual demonstration.**

The Sixth Lesson is a lesson in invocation. It is well to know what we are invoking. Whatsoever we desire we are invoking it, and sooner or later it arrives upon us.

A bar of iron gains magnetic virtue by being placed for a time in a special position. So it is thought that particles of matter arranged and long held in a certain posture may eventually get surcharged with life.

As natural phenomena are mysteriously symbolic of mystical realities we can understand by the example of the bar of iron and the particles of matter how it came to pass that the inspirationally taught mystics of old discovered that the inner vision of a person often giving attention to "*Ain Soph*, the Great Countenance of the Absolute," would charge that person with transfiguring newness of Divine Life in plain manifestation. Great promises have been caught by awakening watchers toward the Vast Vast Countenance of "Him who exalts by his power, none teaching like Him," saying: "Look unto me and live."(Is 45:22) "Seek ye my face and live."(Amos 4:5) "I give life to the faint."(Is 40:29) "And I will reveal unto you the abundance of peace and truth."(Jer. 33:6)

Take a wide, wide view of The Vast Vast. He gives to all people liberally and reproves not. Harsh criticism and lack of generosity hail not from Him, – not Life but the Cause that Life is – not Spirit but the Cause that Spirit is.

We call our relationship to the High Eternal First Cause, inspiration, because is comes along with our inward breathing. "The inspiration of the Almighty gives them understanding."(Job 32:8) We call it Spirit, or Breath of Heaven. Breathe toward me heavenly breath, till all this breathing form of me quickens with breath divine.

Father John of Russia felt the stirring of a breath full of curative elixirs quickening the bread and wine of the Eucharist. He cited cases of bodily healing while partaking of these ether-charged elements. Certain names of old were reputed to liberate the healing elixirs biding forever within the airs we daily breathe never noting their mystic offers: "Why, O humankind, will ye die, having power to partake of the breath of immortality?"

Chapter Six - Understanding of God

The cradle doctrine of the New Age is "Thou God seest me – For I also have looked after Him that seeth me." It was also the cradle doctrine of the earliest Hebrew prophets, announcing the coming together of aristocracy and serfdom in the Christ above the pairs of opposites, rich and poor, bond and free.

Abraham sought the wooing Unseen by looking up and hearing the voice of the Light saying, "The land thou seest, to thee will I give it."(Gen 13:15)

Mystical Science brings the close swinging miracle-working uplands to our attention with perpetual urgings. To the bad and the good among us it declares the same: "Lift up your eyes to the fields white for the harvest."(Jn 4:35) If we keep off the world's fighting ground of good and evil in thought and conduct, the clinches of its estimates of what is good have no yea in us, and its estimates of what is evil find in us no agreement.

Visioning toward the same country Abraham was seeking we swing in with the Miracle-Working Heights. "The land thou seest, to thee will I give it," whispers its unceasing voice. (Gen 13:15) Honor and fortune exist for those who remember that they are in the neighborhood of the Great, wrote the truth-announcing Emerson, keeping step in a mystical moment with Moses, the God-taught law giver, and Ezra the inspired reformer.

Remember that we always look toward an object before thinking it, and it is by having oft recourse by inward viewing that then the mind goes on to know and comprehend – and the body, obedient follower, to show the concrete thereof.

He of highest vision rises highest even among the children of earth. Samuel said, "I am a seer," and he went forth to choose a king for Judah and Israel. Jesse of Bethlehem-Judah was the greatest man among the Hebrews, and his sons the finest specimens of Judean manhood. Abinadab, Eliab, and Shammah were marched before the seer. One had a genius for war, one a genius for statecraft, one for language. What a wonderful gift is language! If your language were right you would be the desideratum of kings' courts. You would stop warfare between Isaac and Ishmael, capital and labor, rich and poor!

The world awaits its master of brotherhood-cohering words. "A right word, how good it is, who can measure the force of a right word?"

Chapter Six - Understanding of God

But Samuel said, No, not one of these for king of Judah and Israel. For the one with genius for war has his inner vision toward men to marshal them for martial triumphs; the one with genius for statecraft has his inner viewing set toward men to place them as heads of tribes and territories, and the one with genius for compelling speech is observant of men's swaying emotions under his spellbinding oratory.

Now their youngest brother David took not much note of men. "Mine eyes are ever toward the Lord," he said, "for he shall pluck my feet out of the net." (PS 25:15) Not what he himself did, but what the Lord on high was doing, was David's aspiration. And the seer anointed David with kingship; and he was the greatest warrior on earth, the greatest statesman, the most victory-awakening speaker: - "The Lord hear thee in the day of trouble – The name of the God of Jacob defend thee – send thee help from the Sanctuary – Strengthen thee out of Zion," (Ps 20:1) was his national rallying cry.

Nothing shall by any means defeat us when we often lift up our eyes to Thee!

Five stands for successful labor, and six stands for success without labor, or the miracle of the Highest ever moving toward us.

The hyacinth bulb planted topside down labors desperately to bloom toward China, and succeeds in making an anemic blossom, pale and small, only a plain imitation of itself were it facing the sunshine and ambrosial morning airs. What does the downward looking hyacinth know of its own sun-facing, non-anemic wide-spreading beauty? So we have never seen a man of the Labor-less Supernal order, facing the "Sun of Righteousness with healing in his wings," (Mal 4:2) until the New Dispensation gave us its good news when he came toward us!

The more we look to *Ain Soph,* the Great Countenance of the Absolute, the Origin of knowing, the more we know of the influence of the close-swinging miracle-working world in its finished beneficence.

"Listen, O isles, unto me; and hearken ye people, from far."(Is 49:1) "I will show thee great and mighty things, which thou knowest not."(Jer 33:3)

Beyond the margins of the mind, supernal Wisdom waits. Over the dayspring of a glory from above, the heavens' mysterious healings are distilling for those who obey the mandate: "Lift up your eyes."(Is 40:26, 49:8, 51:6, 60:4, Jer 3:2) "Look unto Me."(Is 45:22) "I am the Lord that healeth thee."(Ex 15:26)

Chapter Six - Understanding of God

The greatest doctrine announced by the voice of inspiration, is that A Mighty One onlooks us, wooing ever as, "What wilt thou?" "Ask what ye will." (Jn 15:7) "Is anything too hard for Me?"(Gen 18:14)

Who of us, looking up, answers face to face? Who of us holds high converse with the Ruler in the heavens, who says, "To him that orders his conversation aright will I show salvation?"(Ps 50:23)

In ancient mythology the sixth god was Cronus, god of the harvest, with two faces, one glowing white and one glooming dark, according as he set himself to harvest from the heights above or from the depths below.

When the man of Galilee touched the six-stepped throne place by daily converse with what David called the glory above the heavens, such magian effulgence gleamed forth from him that multitudes coming unto him, he healed them every one.

We are all harvesting according to our inward viewings. "Why are ye troubled?" asked Jesus, and "Why do thoughts arise in your hearts?" (Lk 24:38)

We had to wait for the birth of Hegel before we got the scientific answer to that question: "We always look toward an object before thinking it and it is by having oft recourse by inward viewing that then the mind goes on to know and comprehend."

High Mysticism is not a science of right thinking, or right conduct; these are strenuous labors. High Mysticism is the call to look up to *Ain Soph*, the Great Countenance of the Absolute, who orders thoughts and speech and conduct anew. "Behold, I make all things new."(Rev 21:5) "I will return unto that people a new language." (Zeph 3:9) "They shall speak with new tongues."(Mk 16:17)

Our speech always declares the direction of our inward viewing, by the harvest of our life conditions. If we mention the shiftlessness, the sorrows, the sufferings of our neighbors we may experience some unpleasantness of body and of affairs formulated by the inward gazing our verbal descriptions betray. Is it not written that the wages of sin or aberrated vision is death? (Rom 6:23)

Mysticism is not a science of goodness and badness of conduct. It is the science of that which harvests as good or bad conduct. It is the science of the genesis of conduct and the genesis of thoughts. Secret viewings compose their own speech, rouse their own emotions, and formulate their own actions.

Chapter Six - Understanding of God

Our initial and compelling faculty is our inner vision. Vision often God-ward and live anew. So shall the body be like a tree planted by the rivers of water - whose leaf fadeth not."(Ps 1:3) Vision often God-ward so that all affairs also may go well. Gaze often toward Our Father, and all thoughts shall be like morning music. Lift up an inward look now and then, to a country whose ether winds ever raying forth their healing aura are swift remedies for all the world's unhappiness.

The kings of Tyre wore the sardius stone, sixth stone of Revelation, to signify that they had caught a threefold luster by invocation. The sixth stone of Revelation is the luster sardius, symbol of invocation.

By physical invocation, the body may renew with the subtle elixirs that wait to mill within it to strengthen and uplift. The hills open in the daytime and at night pinch into themselves the circumambient vitalizings with which the daytime airs are charged. Then they bring forth grass, herbs, and grains for cattle.

The brain of humanity can open and close into itself the wisdom elixirs: "Lift up your heads, ye gates... the King of glory waits to enter in. Who is the King of glory? The Lord, strong and mighty... The Lord of hosts, he is the King of glory."(Ps 24) There is no part of the body that may not open and indraw the subtler-than-air stimulants that would soon burst forth as strength. This is physical invocation.

The mind is surrounded by distant knowledge that it may draw in by asking, and bursts forth with answers as from unseen teachers. This is mental invocation. The sardius stone stands for mental invocation.

The luster sardius stands for mystical invocation - the way to know new things from the heights above the margins of the mind, where things so far untaught lie awaiting our mystical invocation. Pythagoras said that there are magic, mighty syllables making up an Ineffable Name, key to the mysteries of the universe. "The Ineffable Name is key to the mysteries of the universe." "And the throne had six steps: and I saw in the right hand of him that sat on the throne, a book."

Everyone's name is the book of his equipment, and the use he has made of his name constitutes the influence of his name, or its spirit, or its ghost. Would we not expect that he whose vision had lifted highest, and whose invocations had brought him to highest harvestings would shed the strongest and best influence, or spirit, or ghost, by the calling of his name? He who sat upon the throne, with the book in his right hand, announced to all the world, "The holy ghost, whom the Father will send in my name, he shall teach you all things." (Jn 14:26)

Chapter Six - Understanding of God

Surely the magic name for which Pythagoras was seeking to reveal to him the secrets of the universe must be concealed in the name promised to reveal all things by invocation!

"I wept much,"(Rev 5:4) said John the Revelator, because the world went on so long without noticing that some names are like alabaster boxes of empowering ointment. Break them open by invoking them, and mysterious new influences awake through the body, the mind, and environments.

Paul wrote to the Ephesians that revelations would be granted by the acknowledgment of Jesus Christ. That the eyes of our understanding should open to know the hope they may entertain from the calling of him that has put all things under his feet, with name above every name that is named, not only in this world, but also in that which is to come.

Jesus, who was Christ with the fullness of the Godhead bodily, insisted that His name sheds forth fresh life: "My words (my syllables) are life."(Jn 6:63) "I came that ye might have life."(Jn 10:10) "I am the living bread."(Jn 6:51) "He that eateth me, even he shall live by me."(Jn 6:57)

Only Christ Jesus ever told us how to quicken anew with the life of which our nerves are scant, and He declared that His Name would stir the ether-breaths of the unseen eternal world to inbreathe with our inbreathing

The conclusion of the ancients was that there is no science of wealth or health so great as the science of inbreath.

"An hundred and forty and four thousand had His Father's name in their foreheads," (Rev 14:1) said John, which means that the right number to stir the world shall have cognizance of awakening Spirit, or Holy Ghost, or healing winds, or God breath from heaven that the name of the Lord of Life conveys.

Invocation is the greatest efficiency of prayer. Did not the voice of far past inspiration declare that the name of Deity transcends prayer? Jesus of Nazareth called the Overlooking Deity Father. At the crucifixion He cried, "Father, forgive them!"(Lk 23:34)

Why have we not been taught to lift up our eyes to the prayer-answering, for-giving Father and partake of the same Beneficence into which the glorified Jesus was then gazing? This Beneficence is ever streaming toward us.

Should our children's children be taunted on and on because of the foolhardiness we exhibit today? Though your errors were as scarlet, the for-giving answers to the Jesus Christ prayer on Calvary passing them along to the sin-undoing High Redeemer, they shall be as if they had never been.

"I will set no wicked thing before mine eyes; it shall not cleave to me," was David's song for our instruction. (Ps 101:3)

In the science of numbers, Six is significant of complete manifestation, all the faculties raised to their highest exercise. And sin is errant vision unified with errant words and acts. Errant vision, or sin, carries the banner of triumphant arrival at complete manifestation.

To the mystically wise the badge of triumphant arrival at the worst that downward vision can accomplish, is tantamount to telling plainly the possibilities of upward visioning.

The secret that sin tells to the wise is that by vision toward matter and mind and their laws of pleasure and pain we get caught in the wheel of destruction. But by vision toward the Highest One above the pairs of opposites, we get charged with independence of matter and mind. It is ours to choose whether we will be blooms in the Garden of Immortality here and now, or blooms in the garden of apoplexy and failure.

To the mystic, the sensualist with his blazing sores of malefic contagion, is sign royal of the possibility of one charging himself to fadeless bloom with heavenly inspiration, till people round the globe touch the hem of his garment of healing; till "the gentiles come to his light, and kings to the brightness of his rising."

To the mystic, contagion is sign royal of the possibility that we can be charged with heavenly inspiration.

There is but one commandment issuing from the Giver of Almighty Health, the Author of Strength, and that one commandment, is "Look unto me, and be ye saved, all the ends of the earth."(Is 45:22) "Beside me there is no Savior."(Hos 13:4)

Chapter Six - Understanding of God

Elijah did not touch the sixth mark of arrival at the best that the high watch could do for him, for he did his in-breathing of victorious energy intermittently, and unwittingly. He did his upward watching halfway, unknowing of the secret of up-looking power. Like most people of this very day he spent more time viewing his troubles and describing them, than glorying in the immune splendor of the wisdom-imparting Jehovah.

To the true mystics the upward looking and the breathing in of heavenly atmospheres are volitional and scientific. They know whence the energizing breaths come wafting their newness, and the healing elixirs come streaming with enlivening vigor. They also know that if they are not rounded up with unkillable Omnipotence, it is because they have neglected this science.

The world awaits the sixth mark of unceasing acceptance of the divine Highest only; it awaits the visible bloom of immortality in the Garden of Man – the Jesus point of plain demonstration that "No man taketh my life from me."

In the Apocrypha, we read that in the sixth place the Lord imparts understanding. Understanding imparted from the Lord is the desideratum of all humanity – for having touched this magian flame, life is kindled to glow forever – for understanding is a wellspring of life.

Mystic understanding is strength, identical with divine strength. "I am understanding," said the Lord, (Prov 8:14) "I have strength," (Prov 8:14); and it is written that He gives this strength to his people.

Habakkuk's three mystical chapters tell of the presence of the Lord of demonstration now among us and of our unopened faculties, ready now to quicken to life in every part all who believe in his leadership and his nearness, and call upon his revealing name. "Who hath believed our report?" "That believing, ye might have life through His name." (Jn 20:31) "Call unto me, and I will answer thee, and show thee great and mighty things, which thou knowest not." (Jer 33:3) "And all the nations shall fear and tremble for all the goodness and for all the prosperity that I procure unto it." (Jer 33:9)

Paul was told to rise up quickly, calling upon this name, and knew its ripening value: "I press toward the mark, for the prize of the high calling of God in Christ Jesus, and if in anything ye be other-wise minded, God shall reveal even this unto you."(Phil 3:14-15)

Chapter Six - Understanding of God

Many Christians have been "otherwise minded," in their calling, and have had what they called for revealed in full measure.

This is the practice of the calling principle: "Thou shalt lift up thy face unto God." (Job 22:26) "Thou shalt also decree a thing, and it shall be established unto thee." (Job 22:28) Every choice is a call, direct or implied.

The historic demonstrations of important men give definite cue and clue to each individual's demonstration, on a small or a large scale, according as his choice has been powerful or puny, and his objective glorious or commonplace.

Paul, and the Christians he gathered round him, lifted up their faces to the Almighty, and called to the Victorious One, until they were great conquerors together. "I am more than conqueror," Paul declared of himself (Rom 8:37). And he insisted that the victorious Christ Jesus he had so persistently invoked, charged him so near to the brim with Christ executiveness, that he could work miracles. "I can do all things through Christ which strengthens me." (Phil 4:13)

Paul did not round up to the six mark of unkillable Life and unbreakable Omnipotence, because of getting entangled in a downward watch toward sex differentiations, and foods suitable and unsuitable. He split on the rocks of sex and food. Though on his spiritual flights he proclaimed "neither male nor female in Christ Jesus," (Gal 3:28) yet he suffered not a woman to speak in the Christian Church.

Though on his vision's scientific formulas he read plainly that, "Neither if we eat are we better, not if we eat not are we worse," (I Cor 8:8) yet he became explicit in explaining what might and what might not be eaten, and forbade any man who was not a strenuous worker to eat anything at all; as though eating were very important.

The glory of sin is its consistency – it keeps at its own stride toward full arrival and nothing diverts it from its six mark's grand completeness. Does any upward watcher catch heavenly health by his persistence heavenward, until his health breaks forth like the morning, and every sick person catches health from him, as surely as the downward watcher, who, identifying with small pox, gives them to his neighbors, if they come into contact with him? It is only the Jesus among us of whom is it yet written, "Multitudes came unto him, and he healed them every one."(Matt 15:30) "But as many as received him, to them gave he power to visibly become the sons of God."(Jn 1:12)

Chapter Six - Understanding of God

In mysticism we learn the law of our subtle visional sense. We find that we use our inner vision constantly, and we find that our thoughts follow its wake, and that physical conditions follow the thoughts. For whatever is looked toward as an objective to the inner eye reveals its secrets, whether the lofty One inhabiting Eternity, or the motives of our neighbors. There is but one law running along to the flowering of all steadfast visioning.

"The secret of the Lord is with them that fear him." (Ps 25:14) Fear is singleness of eye. "In the fear of the Lord is the instruction of wisdom." (Prov. 9:10) "The fear of the Lord is a fountain of life." (Prov. 14:27) There is no want to them that fear him. Fear, or singleness of eye toward any objective, is disclosure of its secrets, and experience of its working power.

Peter discovered that there is great effect from singleness of eye toward names, as toward other objectives, and he chose the Name of the Savior of humanity to stand by.

Micah got it as an unfailing law, that, "My name shall cause to see that which is." (Mic 6:9) Peter proved it by walking with the angels, and doing their works, after fearing the "only Name given under heaven, whereby men must be saved."(Acts 4:12) For as the angels do wondrously, so also did Peter wondrously always by the power of the name he inbreathed.

The purpose of religion has always been to teach people to make the most of themselves. At its highest point of instruction, it has taught that right thought and right conduct follow right view. To look steadfastly toward the Helper, and Healer, and Savior abiding unseen but always within calling distance, has ever been its injunction: endure, "as seeing Him who is invisible."(Heb 11:27)

There is one operative virtue running through all things. All things super-celestial may be drawn into the celestial, and all things supernatural may be drawn into the natural.

By much attention to material things, we make such drafts on matter that its mysterious operations seize upon us in more than conceivable abundance. We suck in the way of matter, by indirect calling, as we look to it for our welfare and our knowledge.

Chapter Six - Understanding of God

Let us volitionally lift up our eyes to the Sender of the mystic cure and make all our drafts on these immortal streams and the mysteries of health, and prosperity, and incessant renewal shall be revealed and experienced. Jesus having demonstrated this was able to declare, "Whatsoever ye shall ask in my name that will I do." (Jn 14:13) "Ask what ye will, and it shall be done unto you," for "all things are delivered unto me of my Father." (Matt 11:27)

The Science of God reveals all science. The true Name of God reveals the Science of God. It reveals all names – from the names of the stars – to the names of the insects – from the names of the fearless archangels – to the right names for the victorious earth walk of our children.

The name of one, Jesus Christ, who knows the Great Revealing Name, reveals his knowledge. "The Holy Ghost, whom the Father will send in my name, he shall teach you all things." (Jn 14:26) "Thou holdest fast my name" (Rev 2:13) "I will give a new name which no man knoweth save he that receiveth it."(Rev 2:17)

All that we know yet of the Maker of the universe, is the practice of His Presence. Of His actual substance and purposes, we know nothing. "Touching the Almighty we cannot find him out" (Job 37:23) – "with him is terrible majesty." (Job 37:22)

Yet Elihu found the Almighty teaching and exalting him, and giving him songs in the night, as the result of his upward watch and the in-breath of the Almighty that awakened the God-Seed of understanding within him.

Elihu seemed to know no other name of the Highest but God. But he spoke of a messenger, an interpreter, a ransom, an atonement one who could enlighten with living light.

By the recognition of the atonement, we should begin to breathe in flakes of joy and wisdom from the Giver of Wisdom. The recognition of the Man of atonement makes draft on the Holy Spirit, "The Holy Spirit whom the Father will send in my name." (Jn 14:26) It makes draft on life: "I will put my spirit in you and ye shall live." (Eze 37:5) "Wherefore turn yourselves, and live ye." (Eze 18:32) The Holy Spirit is the ghost or spirit of wholeness; or breath of wholeness.

Job knew that to regard the breath he breathed as the Healing Spirit, instead of common atmospheric air, and never to speak of the outcome as anything but

Chapter Six - Understanding of God

transforming, would fetch him out on to some upland that those who breathed just air, and called it air, would never reach.

And he was right. His witness in the heavens, and his breath, always known by him while inbreathing it as the God breath, brought him to where he was blessed beyond his calculations. With mysterious wisdom, he knew himself well pleasing to the High Eternal.

The Apostles of the Regeneration knew the name of the Atonement. They knew their breath as charged with the ether wafts of healing. They knew the law of the vision, and the re-born status that was to be the outcome.

This was their Christianity. In the name of the Great Achiever, they drew their breath as the Holy Spirit, which is the spirit of wholeness, and they were transformed characters. They walked in the fourth dimension in space. No prison walls could hold them, and no lions' jaws could destroy them. No former ignorance or common birth among the people who breathed common air, and sought their life from material productions could count against their being the wisest men on earth.

They took up a life near us and yet above us, a life with the power of manifestation here and there, and now and then, throughout the generations, not unmet even in the present century.

But their mode of arrival at the state of just people made perfect, on the unseen plane, is not the final arrival that mystical interpretation foretells.

To be charged to overflowing with irresistible miracle-working power, while yet manifest in the flesh; to be the radiance of buoyant joy while yet walking among the children of earth. To shed the perfume of healing and strengthening and illuminating while yet speaking with us and smiling upon us is the final Christian ministry. This is the bloom of full obedience to the Sacred Edict, "Look unto Me." (Is 45:22) There is no warfare where the vision of God is. There is no disease where the healing Name is called. There is no inadequacy or failure while the Spirit of God is in the nostrils, inbreathed as the only breath. This is living truth.

If we would transcend our limitations, we must look above our limitations. We always believe in what we look toward; and we draw what we believe in. Deep believers in punishment are unconsciously drawing it. All the prophets drew

Chapter Six - Understanding of God

punishment. Great believers in miracles draw them. Some drew Pentecostal tongues, and spoke languages by the Holy Spirit they had never studied.

The watch of the first Christian Apostles was toward the Lamb that in the midst of the throne is the unfailing Provider; and they wanted for nothing. All those who gathered to them were abundantly supplied.

Their vision was toward the Highest, and no one could set upon them to hurt them, with power to defeat them, nor hurt the thousands obeying their injunction to continue in prayer and watch in the same. Their faces were set toward the Author of peace, and they allowed no one to be a slayer of himself or his fellowmen. Their look was toward Christ the Triumphant, and no one could grovel in their presence. No one could lack joy. No one was foolish. They were the spiritual magistral, or sovereign remedy, answering the prayers of the ancients for a way of universal cure – opiate divine to the sorrows of the world.

The High and Lofty One inhabiting Eternity is above the pairs of opposites, good and evil, life and death, spirit and matter, therefore his ways that inspire us as we look toward Him are not our accustomed ways. We let Spirit go on its free way, to leave us poor in spirit; we are independent of Good; we do not hug tightly to Life, as though it were precious. For Spirit, Good, and Life, are gifts of the Highest.

Shall we be in love with gifts who stand for the gifts of the Highest instead of the Highest? It is not the gifts of the Highest that say, "Look unto Me and be ye saved," (Is 45:22) though all the gifts of the Highest do come if we set our inner eye toward them and call their names, drafting on their waiting offers.

Can we not call sleep, and inbreathe sleep, that subtle thing that the beloved of God receive, till insomnia flees our being? But sleep is not God. Sleep is a gift of God. To joy in sleep is to be like Isaiah's people rejoicing in a harvest of grass and apples. The bloom of sleep is not the perfume of unspoilable health shedding itself abroad from the sleeper.

We can call strength, inbreathing its offered vigors, looking toward its omnipresent smile, till strength nerves us to masterful handling of lions and elephants. But strength by itself is not God. Strength is a gift of God.

To joy in strength is to joy as in a harvest of apples that lose their flavor, or corn that moulds. For all the gifts, sought with eagerness for their own sake, have their

Chapter Six - Understanding of God

round of existence and disappearance, and those who receive them partake of the same. But thou! O Highest Original! art forever, and the manna Thou givest for the calling of Thy name, is radiant beneficence scattering and yet increasing, till the world is alive forevermore!

The choice of the High Original alone instructs the mind, renews the body, engirds the affairs. "Call unto me, and I will answer thee," (Jer 33:3) and revive my Spirit in thee, and "nothing shall prevail against thee."(Jer 15:20)

Nothing prevailed against Jesus. "I can both lay down my life and take it up," (Jn 10:17-18) He said. He knew all things, and needed not that any man should teach Him. His face was always heavenward, comrading always with the King of Kings and Lord of Lords.

Thus invoking the name of him calls toward us his masterfulness of life and death, knowledge and ignorance, health and sickness, majesty and insignificance. Has it not always been believed that invoking the name of a man of masterfulness and courage inbreathes masterfulness and courage? And calling sleep brings it? And calling the invisible goods with which the spaces are charged fetches them?

Call to the trees that lean and whisper against the far horizons, and they shall tell thee all their secrets, from the cedars of Lebanon to the hyssop that springs on the wall. Call to the stars that lie on their black beds through the long north lights, and they shall tell thee what the schools have not discovered.

Call to the Lord of Life and Glory beyond the bars of human sense, and all the living fountains lying deep in thee shall quicken into stirring streams. All the pent-up wisdom that inhabits you shall leap to meet the Universal Wisdom, shining forth as the sun with the glory of their Father. "There is none like unto thee, O Lord! Thou art great, and thy name is great in might!"(I Chr 29:11-12)

The disciples had associated with the Risen Christ until they knew that He had borne the griefs and carried the sorrows of all the human race. Because of His God Substance it had been as nothing to Him, therefore "opened he their understanding, that they might understand the Scriptures." (Lk 24:45) He dissolved the bars of human ignorance that hid their Lord-implanted inward wisdom. He dissolved cold foolishness and dark ignorance by the hot beams of His bright Righteousness, or shining Understanding.

Chapter Six - Understanding of God

The Risen Christ was weightless of body and think-less of mind. He was Pure Understanding, hot with universal dissolvent to human heaviness, dewy with working mystery. Then was fulfilled in His disciples the inspired promise that they of understanding should do exploits. Then was fulfilled in them the promise that whosoever should draw out his soul to the hungry, and satisfy the afflicted, should have his light shine forth in obscurity, and the Lord should guide him continually.

"To satisfy the afflicted" (Is 58:10) is to acknowledge the Lord of affliction. The Lord of affliction was Jesus the Judean, wounded for the transgressions of the world, bruised for its iniquities, bearing the chastisement of the peace of all humanity that by his stripes they might be healed.

To draw out the soul, or to acknowledge it, are noted as identical activities in the Scriptures. They have the same results: the breaking forth of the light, and the consciousness of daily guidance by the Lord of victorious living. "In all thy ways acknowledge Him, and He shall direct thy paths." (Prov 3:6) "Draw out thy soul to the hungry, and satisfy the afflicted…then shall thy light rise in obscurity, and thy darkness be as the noonday: And the Lord shall guide thee continually." (Is 58:10-11)

To acknowledge the Great Hungry is a mystical expression, meaning to acknowledge Him that swallows up death, and hell. It is to acknowledge Jesus the Savior from death, and Hades, and darkness and the paths downward.

The only Scripture the Risen One gave the disciples, after their acknowledgment of His vicarious achievement, was His own name. "The Holy Spirit whom the Father will send in my name shall teach you all things." (Jn 14:26) And to the world at large he prophesied: "Ye shall not see me henceforth, till ye shall say, blessed is he that cometh in the name of the Lord." (Matt 23:39)

No library on earth holds a book guaranteeing to teach all things. But the ancient wise men declared that there is an Ineffable Name that teaches the mysteries of the universe.

But Jesus himself testified for all time: "The Holy Spirit whom the Father will send in my name shall teach you all things." (Jn 14:26) "In my name preach the gospel, heal the sick, cast out devils, raise the dead." (Matt 10:8)

Chapter Six - Understanding of God

He knew the Ineffable Name that is key to the mysteries of the universe. He also knew that whoever should keep His Name as Jesus Christ should come into the Ineffable Name.

"Thou holdest fast my name. I will give a new name."(Rev 2:13) This new name cannot be spoken without instantly accomplishing the raising of the dead or the healing of the sick, or the illuminating of the life. It can never be spoken in vain. "Thou shalt not take the name of the Lord thy God in vain," (Ex 20:7) is a prophecy, just like "They shall not hurt or kill in all my holy mountain." (Is 11:9)

All the so-called commandments are prophetic utterances, to the initiated. They all mean that when the Ineffable Name of the Lord is known, we are at home in the perfect land, where the former things come not into mind any more.

A Kabalistic system made the name Jesus the equivalent of *Jehovah Shammain*, or the saving Word; and some studied the two syllables as in themselves the Ineffable Name.

Many can testify that the name Jesus Christ is a mysterious power although he is more often regarded as the historic sufferer rather than the victorious Peace-Presence.

Notice the testimony of a woman who had been converted to Christianity and had been poisoned by her angry relative to put her out of their way as being their religious disgrace. Having read that in his name the dead should rise, and if a Christian should drink any deadly thing it should not hurt them, she began to call the name. She persistently invoked it though the well-known symptoms of mortal hurt were increasing. Suddenly she felt as if a stream of pure water were flowing through her body. It kept on with mysterious swiftness, till every vestige of the poison was eliminated, and new life began pulsing through her being.

Who now is ignoring every disastrous state of affairs, and separating himself to the one name by which the first Apostles wrought their miracles?

"And the throne had six steps. And I saw in the right hand of him that sat upon the throne, a book." (Rev 5:1) "I wept much," wrote John the Apocalyptic seer, "because no man was found worthy to open and to read the book."(Rev 5:4)

Chapter Six - Understanding of God

It is the book effecting by the mysterious writing on its covering, the unlocking of the doors of limitation, and the uniting of whoever reads the outer writing to unstinted blessings.

"Seek ye out of the book of the Lord and read, no one of these shall fail. – For the deaf shall hear the words of the book, and the eyes of the blind shall see out of obscurity, and out of darkness."(Is 29:18)

Surely, the book in the right hand of the Lamb, slain for the transgressions of the race, gives for its outer reading the name or revealing so vitally insisted upon by the first Christian Apostles – and so ignored as to its mystical potency by the Christians of today. The opening of its inner writing waits upon the faithful reading of its outer form. "Blessed is he that readeth," (Rev 1:3) "I will give him to eat of the hidden manna."(Rev 2:17)

Faithful reading is always associated with understanding: "Whereby when ye read, ye may understand my knowledge in the mystery of Christ." (Eph 3:4) "Whoso readeth, let him understand."(Matt 24:15)

And understanding is mystical light. It is the light pent up and hidden in all humanity as it was in the first disciples of Jesus. It is the glorious light of the Lord of the wide universe. "Then shall thy light break forth as the morning"(Is 58:8) "And the Lord shall be unto thee an everlasting light."(Is 60:19)

The same law of light reigns for the unseen shining as for the manifest. Do not scientists insist that the same light that illuminates the noon-day sky is present in the darkened chamber? And that the bars of hiding being removed - the light within springs to meet the light without?

The breaking forth of the pent-up light, which is our hidden understanding, is associated with the bursting forth of our pent-up health: "Then shall thy light break forth as the morning, and thine health shall spring forth speedily."(Is 58:8)

It is associated with rising: "Unto you that fear my name, shall the sun of righteousness arise, with healing in his wings," (Mal 4:2) "And the gentiles shall come to thy light, and kings to the brightness of thy rising." (Is 60:3)

"Tarry ye in the city of Jerusalem," said the Risen Lord, "till ye be endued with power from on high." (Lk 24:49) "Ye shall receive power after that the Holy Ghost is come upon you."(Acts 1:8) "The Holy Ghost whom the Father will send in my name." (Jn 14:26)

Then the obedient disciples tarried in Jerusalem. They tarried during the forty days of the Lord's ten appearances, plus the days to the fully come Pentecost, the Sixth day of Sivan, the feast of the harvest; coming together often, with one accord, to call upon the Spirit-imbuing name. On the sixth day of Sivan, the house where they were gathered trembled in the rushing Spirit they had invoked by their persistent calling. Tongues of mystic fire whispered to them the powerful mysteries. They were ready to greet the outside world with a new ministry.

Six is the number consecrated to final equipment for heavenly offices. No equipment transcends the effulgence that wakes in us the healing word, the tongue for speech with angels. Even the shadow of Peter, most name-distraught, caused joyous forgetfulness of pain.

Jerusalem is symbol of the Self. To tarry at the Self, invoking the Name that wakes magian majesty – inbreath immortalizing – medicine of God is labor worthy of the sons and daughters of humanity.

Jesus of Judea set His vision toward the Author of Success, and inbreathed the airs of Paradise. He opened the gates between Himself and unstinted transcendence. Jesus rose to immortality, and His Name is full of life-giving, miracle-working energy; it opens the gates between humankind and its native kingship.

Choose this day the objective for your vision's oft-time gaze, and your calling's precious good. Be as hotly intent as Jesus toward God.

Practice

Bible Verses to commit to memory

> ➢ "In him was life; and the life was the light of men."(Jn 1:4)

> ➢ "All things are delivered unto me of my Father." (Matt 11:27)

> ➢ "And whatsoever ye shall ask in my name that will I do." (Jn 14:13)

> ➢ "That whatsoever ye shall ask of the Father in my name, he may give it to you." (Jn 15:16)

Chapter Six - Understanding of God

> ➤ "Thy name is as ointment poured forth."(Cant 1:3)

> ➤ "I press toward the mark of the prize of the high calling of God in Christ Jesus – if in anything ye be otherwise minded God shall reveal, even this to you." (Phil 3:14,15)

> ➤ "Call unto me, and I will answer thee, and show thee great and mighty things which thou knowest not." (Jer 33:3)

> ➤ "The Holy Ghost, whom the Father will send in my name, shall teach thee all things." (Jn 14:26)

> ➤ "I have made thee like unto Him, even God, who quickeneth the dead, and calleth those things which be not as though they were." (Rom 4:17)

Résumé - Saturday & Sunday First Week

When the disciples had associated with the Risen Christ long enough, to sense that he had been wounded for the transgressions of a world, and that by acknowledgment of the same the world might go free, - "then opened he their understanding that they might understand the Scriptures."(Lk 24:25) And the Scriptures he gave them was his own name: "The Holy Ghost whom the Father will send in my name shall teach you all things."(Jn 14:26)

This name constitutes the most remarkable book ever mentioned on earth, for the Spirit of Truth it wakens, shall guide into all truth, and show humankind of things to come (Jn 16:13).

Every name conveys the bearer's qualities, and when called earnestly, imbues the caller with those qualities. If he is a strong intellect, the repetition of his name, especially the calling of his name earnestly, imbues the caller with new intellectual strength.

Cruden, in his immortal Concordance, under the heading of *Call*, declares that things which had no existence may come into sight by strong words of calling, I have made thee like unto Him, even God, who quickeneth the dead, and calleth those things which be not as though they were."(Rom 4:17) "Who has God so nigh unto them as the Lord our God is in all things that we call unto Him for?" (Deut 4:7) Isaiah lamented that no man called for justice (Is 59:4)

Chapter Six - Understanding of God

The giving-forth power of some names has been known for centuries. Canon Farrar, in his Life of Christ, says it would be well for us if we were to pick up that old well known law and practice it.

Surely, by this law, the man who has shown the most super human power must confer the most super human powers through his name. Therefore the disciples of Jesus Christ became the most wonderful Apostles of doctrine that the world has ever known; for no man's name ever named stands for such colossal achievements as Christ Jesus whom they spent so many weeks calling upon.

John the Revelator had been among the callers, and he knew that the little book in the right hand of him that sat upon the throne (Rev 5) was the name, Jesus Christ.

"The throne had six steps."(I Kings 10:19) Six is the number of attainment to spiritual insight, or illumination above the brain. It is often rendered understanding. We can know a great deal, be mathematicians, linguists, dialecticians, without this brightness of the Over-Soul shining upon our words and deeds. Man can be so full of mathematics that other men will round the globe to sit at his feet for instruction. This is the meaning of "six" – i.e., throneship.

A person can be so full of epidemic that whosoever but touches the hem of their garment may be cast down into a bed of sickness. Has any one seen a man so full of the contagion of God that whosoever touched his raiment was instantly healed, and now sheds abroad health like a contagion?

Saul was told to call upon the name Jesus Christ (Acts 22). His name was changed to Paul, and his aprons and handkerchiefs were full of the contagion of God. (Acts 19) "As many as touched Jesus were made whole."(Matt 4:36). Whosoever stepped into the shadow of Peter, calling on Jesus Christ, was healed. (Acts 5:15)

There was a contagion ready to burst forth in the name of Jesus Christ in old days. That contagion still exists, but there is either curiosity mixed with doubt, or pure doubt without curiosity, in the minds of all who are now told to call upon it, to cry sharply upon it.

The name is like an alabaster box that has to be sharply broken open in order that the precious ointment may be obtained. Is it not written "Thy name is as ointment poured forth?"(Cant 1:3)

Chapter Six - Understanding of God

We will choose the name of the one who wrought forth power over earth and heaven, and in whose name is folded the new name with new powers in it. (Rev. 2:17) We will choose the name of Him who has redeemed us out of every nation. (Rev 5)

To sight toward an object with fixed, steady attention and call its name is to be related to it in the end. We must give our strict attention to something supernally worthwhile.

Let us take Saturday and Sunday to call upon the name Jesus Christ. As the Jews gathered the same portion of manna for Saturday and Sunday so we will gather the manna promised to fall in the calling of that name. (Rev.2)

It is the name above every name, said Paul. (Eph.1) "Far above all rule and dominion, and above every name that is named, not only in this age but also in that which is to come." (Eph 1:21) We will stretch up our hands and cry to that name. "Does not Wisdom cry?" (Prov 8) Let us declare our great need, for he answers, What wilt thou? He has promised, "Whatsoever ye shall ask in my name, that will I do."(Jn 14:13).

There is an ineffable name, the key to the mysteries of the universe. According to the Christian Scriptures, the name Jesus Christ is that revealing name, key to all understanding.

Whatever we look toward, we come into identification with. They who seek Me identify with Me. They reign with Me. They live as My life, they strengthen as My strength, they understand as My understanding. What I Am, they are. They call upon My victorious Name, and whatsoever they do prospers, reminding humanity of My ever present, ever friendly, ever available Supremacy. For I send the Healing Ghost, the Enwisdoming Breath, to them who call My Miracle-Working Name – Christ Jesus – bursting through which is the other Name, only known to them that invoke My Anointing Name.

The Radiant "I AM"

By Emma Curtis Hopkins, Teacher of Teachers

The listening disciple becomes a preaching apostle. Standing at the Center of Being and looking outward over the world, instruction is received from every quarter. But who has told himself that all the objects he beholds and all their movements are but projections of his own judgment? He seems always to be a learner and a seeker till at the center of his consciousness the fact is suddenly proclaimed that he himself produced the world as it appears.

Then he no longer listens to information from without; he authorizes from within himself what he would see and hear and touch; even what he would know.

I have been a listening disciple. I have let people and objects and activities come toward me and impinge upon me till I have been over-piled and mountain-covered with thoughts. But now, I know that I AM at my own Center, authority over and through my universe. I shall ordain my twelve disciples, or my twelve powers, to spread my Original Nature abroad till from me to the utmost stretches all is my Divine Ego.

It is the teaching that all is Spirit, and that matter is only the obedient shadow-picturing thereof, which is the final subtle message toward me that makes me see that I AM what I AM and alter not. Spirit is the gentle Mother doctrine among the doctrines of the worlds, gentle but inexorable. She brings to exposure the Man-Child, my I AM, who shall rule all nations with a rod of iron. The iron that is strongest is magnetic. It rules in the earth by holding all the particles together. It rules in the sun. It rules in all the spheres. They roll because of the magnet. So all my being has moved because of my I AM. So all my universe shall wheel to my ordination.

This is my ministry. I am glad to give my self to my divine Self and to give all my world to my divine Self and let my divine Self do in judgment twelve works upon the earth.

This is my ministry. I have heard all I shall ever hear. I know all I shall ever know. I now make my divine Self known.

I make my divine Self known by speaking, thinking, writing and living the word of my divine Self - my I AM. I reign from sea to sea and from the river to the uttermost parts of the earth. I reign by my knowledge of my own I AM and its last name. The name of my I AM in the days of the manifestation of a universe, which I made by speaking from my Central Point, is Jesus Christ. The I AM in me is Jesus Christ. I speak boldly of my divine Self to the world in which I walk. I think from my divine Self forward over its surface through all its substance. I write what I know and I write what I AM, and what I write is the fiber of all things.

They shall feel themselves knitting into transfigured embodiments by my written words. "What you see, write in a book and send it to the seven churches." (Rev 1:11)

I live as a breath of life forward and back through the universe. I AM the conduct of my world. What I do it does. Conducting from my Center, I satisfy my world with what I AM. My world can find no flaw in me. I can find no flaw in my divine Self. Because I live at my Center, you live also. My rod of iron is my being what I AM and knowing it.

"We give thanks to thee, O Lord God Almighty, who is and was, because thou hast taken to thyself thy great power and hast reigned." (Rev 12:17) These that are thankful are my powers. I AM Lord God Almighty to my own powers.

I AM the power of Life to the universe. Because I live, all that has form or name shall live. There shall be no death, nor fear of death throughout the boundaries of eternal spaces from this day forth forever. That which proceeds forth from me is Life and the power of Life forever. As I breathe, the creatures of the sea and air and sands rise up refreshed and there is no power against their life and no ending of their life forever from this day forth.

I AM the unending, irresistible Life of the world. I think this…. I speak this…. I write this…. I live this. This is my ministry, which I AM. "And we will give ourselves continually to prayer and to the ministry of the word." (Acts 6:4)

I AM the power of Health to the universe. Because I AM holy at my Center, I make whole wherever I decree. I AM authority. There shall be happy, joyous, free, fearless Health through this universe from this day. All that have name and shape shall this day lift up their heads with new refreshment. The elixirs of a fadeless healing shall steal through them. There shall be no disease or sickness from this day of the Lord onward. "And the inhabitants shall not say, I am sick…" (Is 33:24)

The Radiant "I AM"

I AM the unending, irresistible, beautiful Health of the whole universe. I, its Center, shed my Health abroad. This is my stop-less ministry. I think this…. I speak this…. I write this…. I live this….

I AM the power of strength to the universe. Because I AM unalterable, I AM omnipotence. I minister myself abroad. All that have shape or name feel stealing through them a reviving strength from this day which nothing shall ever interfere with. I strengthen wherever I decree. I AM Authority. There shall be lifting up and strong godliness throughout all mysteries of height and depth and plain and valley from this day onward. There shall no faintness seize upon anything. There shall no weakness touch anything. There shall no feebleness be heard of forever and forever. The prophecy is fulfilled in me which reads, "When men are cast down, thou shalt say, there is lifting up." (Job 22:29)

I AM the Strength of the universe. This is my ministry. Strength that proceeds from me is irresistible, unending. I think this… I speak this… I write this… I live this… I AM a tower whose radiance is elixir for infinity.

I AM the power of Support to the universe. Everything that has shape or name is upborne and prospered in all its ways from this day on. There shall be no lack or disappointed effort. All shall rise and have self-respect from this day on. I from my Center AM a radiance of upbearing sustainment through all this universe. There shall be no poverty, no lack, no want from this day forth.

I AM the Sufficiency of my universe. It is my decree. The elixir of bounty, of prospering effort, spreads forth from me. This is my irresistible, unending ministry. I think this… I speak this… I write this… I live this…

I AM a tower whose radiance sheds abroad Protection for infinite kingdoms. That which speeds forth as my radiance is the Holy Spirit of Revelation. I AM the unending peaceable defense of the whole universe. By Me, all that have name or shape are safe and secure running, or walking, or flying forever. They shall not fear. They shall not be attacked. They shall not be hurt. The days of hurting have flown away. The dreams of danger are past. Things wake as my mighty elixirs spread through them borne on the streams of my word, my thought, my writings, my life breaths. They rouse themselves. They are safe forevermore. "They shall not hurt or kill or destroy in all my holy mountain." (Is 11:9)

The Radiant "I AM"

I AM the Security of the infinite stretches and of the near creations. "Peace, peace to them that are afar off and to them that are near." (Eph 2:17) This is my ministry. I think this…. I speak this…. I write this…. I live this….

I AM the power of Mind to my universe. Even the stones shed a message intelligible to all other shapes and names because of my being the Intelligence of all things shedding my nature forth without stopping. No foolishness or ignorance shall ever shame anything visible or invisible from this day on forever. Its Presence is its wisdom. Its Presence is its information. An elixir of intelligence is on its stop-less march from me at my Center forever through all the reaches of space and formulation. I decree Intelligence. I decree Mind. I think and all the universe thinks divinely like Me. My Mind is not as the former mind which could change or stop. It is the Jesus Christ Mind, whose word shall not pass away.

I AM a tower whose radiance is unending Wisdom through all things. This is my ministry, my Logos. I think this… I speak this… I write this… I live this… I AM the radiant Logos in Mind.

I AM the power of Speech to my universe. My tongue is its tongue. What I say, it says from its smallest atom to its gigantic formulation. My Central Name is my tongue of radiance. All that speak, speak of the I AM. One tongue only shall speak. Its language, no man or stone did hear nor could ever hear till I should speak from my Center. I now speak what I speak from my Jesus Christ Name. So atoms and angels speak a new heaven and a new earth into their own view, empowered by my tongue with its elixirs of fire. I speak and the universe utters itself.

I AM a tower whose radiance sheds eloquent Speech through atoms and man. This is my ministry. I think this… I speak this… I write this…I live this…

I AM the power of Writing, Recording, Witnessing of Jesus Christ, and the Name folded within the gates of that Name. What I write the world writes. I fix my hallowed glory with my fingers and all things fix themselves to go no more away from their home forever. The Written Word is the haven of man and of beast. I AM the inspiring pen of the world. I shall find my inspiration everywhere. Nothing unlike my writing lives. All except my inspirations vanish. I AM from my Center the fixing and transfixing pen. I shall not faint or fail to fix my glory everywhere. I AM man's inspiration with his pen and I inspire all things to record me as I AM. I AM a tower whose radiance is the inspiration to pen itself in its divinity in every shape and name through infinity. I think this… I speak this… I write this… I live this…

The Radiant "I AM"

I AM the power of Song. Joyous Song, that steals in unquenchable smiling through the universe. I AM the Eternal Smile. As I shed my Self through the atoms and through the globes, they sing. I AM the joyous song, unquenchable, unhinderable, forever. No other sound but singing, no other voice but joy is heard from this day forth.

I AM the inspiring joy of my world forever. This is my ministry. I think this.... I speak this.... I write this.... I live this. There is joy beyond ecstasy. I AM that joy.

I AM the power of Skill for all things. From me there steals forever a quick touch of skillfulness through all fingers. No child needs to be schooled, no bird needs a teacher, and no angel needs a helper. All can do their part and they can do what they will to do. There is no incompetence or need of learning from this day on forever, anywhere.

I AM a tower whose radiance is a skill-inspiring elixir, stop-less, eternal. This is my ministry. I think this... I speak this... I write this... I live this...

I AM the power of Beauty and Judgment. From my poised place, I AM the poise of the ages of men. I judge, and my judgment is what all things go by. They judge like me. I set the features of things into balance and this is their beauty. I balance the atoms that flow in the skin and its balance is its beauty. I set the inner parts into harmony by being the central judgment of eternal facts.

I decree and there is no injustice. Nothing falls into mistake. Nothing is unjust. The scales of my judgment are the scales in the hearts of all men. They will not fail to use these scales. And thus, order and beauty reign from Pole Star to Southern Cross and from right-hand to left of the worlds beyond worlds. "He shall not faint or fail till He hath established judgment in the earth!" (Jer 23:5) I AM a scale whose rods are the beams of unbreakable right. My judgment is right judgment. As I judge, so it is.

All the poise that I AM, I radiate through the universe and all things feel the joy of adjustment. This is my ministry. This is my nature. I think this... I speak this... I write this... I live this...

I AM the power of Heaven to every atom and to every archangel. From my Jesus Christ Center of Being, I shed Heaven through the spaces. All things breathe of my radiance. I shed my Self abroad in unending beauty; Heaven breaks in the heart and on the vision from me to all things, through all things. The old heaven and earth sink

The Radiant "I AM"

away into forgotten dreams because I have found my Self, because I know my Self, because I AM my Self. I have taken up the authority I had from before the worlds were spun on the ethers of time.

I decree Heaven and Heaven it is. My will is done on earth and it is all Heaven. My Kingdom is come and it is the new land of delight that steals on the vision and reaches the senses of all things. Nothing like the dreams of earth, nothing like the motions of matter, ever reaches my universe. As silently as a moonbeam lights on a mountain, so silently has Heaven stolen on the gazes of all the creations of infinity.

I AM a tower whose elixirs of radiance reveal the visions of Heaven to the senses of man. From my Jesus Christ Center I AM Heaven from this day forth to all the universe. This is my stop-less, everlasting ministry. I do this…. I AM this…. My Name is a folding gate that opens and there is no sound. My Name is Jesus Christ, and in that Name I AM the Heaven of all this universe.

Its meaning is its influence. I AM its meaning, its influence, its heavenliness. I think this… I speak this… I write this… I live this… I AM what I AM… I do what I AM by knowing my divine Self as Jesus Christ the Heaven-sending Center of Being, the Heaven-sending Me.

The Radiant "I AM"

Class Notes Volume I

The Mysticism of Emma Curtis Hopkins, Teacher of Teachers

Week One – Realizing the Christ within

By Ute Maria Cedilla

Class Notes

Chapter One - The Silent Edict

1st Gate - **There is Good for me. My Good is my God my Life, my Truth, my Love, my Substance, my Intelligence, Omnipresent, Omnipotent, Omniscient.**

The High and Lofty One inhabiting Eternity invites humanity to look unto His Countenance shining as the sun with healing strength. This is the way of salvation from sin, sickness, misfortune and death.

Isaiah understood it as a Soundless Mandate: "Look unto me and be ye saved all the ends of the earth." (Is 45:22)

Ezekiel understood it as the law of repentance: "Repent and turn away your faces from all your abominations." (Ez 14:6)

Jesus called it the Watch: "What I say unto you, I say unto all, Watch!" (Mk 13:37)

What we vision steadily with our inner eye, causes our thinking. It is high time we set this sense toward God. We will choose the "Great, the Mighty God, great in counsel and mighty in work," (Jer 32:19) for our objective.

This is the way of being God-taught and divinely guided: "I will instruct thee and teach thee in the way which thou shall go; I will guide thee with mine eye." (Ps 32:8)

This is the way we receive new fresh Truth – the resistless Truth of the Eternal Heights.

If the vision is upward, we receive heavenly fervor – the heart flames up with new zeal, new ardor, and new love.

We cannot help encountering new life as we seek our highest Good at the highest Source. The disciples felt their hearts burn on the road to Emmaus when they, as a result of their upward watch, encountered their Lord and Master, Jesus the Christ.

Class Notes

For those high-watchers who know that their true provisions and true positions come straight from above, competition and strenuousness cease, for the Countenance that shines hot with healing tenderness and rich giving is of more value than all that can possibly come through human endeavor.

Lifting the inner eye to Him who is above reason lights the two outer eyes to see the world in a new aspect, gives the tongue new descriptions, and tips the pen with fadeless phrases. The transfiguration of matter waits upon the flawless ecstasy, which only the mystic eye can find.

This deathless visional faculty is our only achieving power. All we have to give is our attention - for what we see that too become we must: God if we see God, dust if we see dust.

Obeying the sublime mandate, "Look unto me," we sense the mystery of redemptive energy.

John tells us that the redeemed are given two songs or two perpetually recurring Names – the Song of Moses and the Song of the Lamb (Rev 15:3)

The Name of the Highest, the Absolute, the Origin of Being, Might and Majesty…. this Name was the song of Moses. It has no reference to benefits or works. It stands by itself alone. It is applied to no other but One. It is I AM that I AM.

The Name I AM that I AM, addressed to the Highest wakens the spirit of authority, majesty, and undefeatable courage, in the breast of even the meekest and weakest.

The Name, I AM that I AM, brings up from the deepest wells of hidden strength in all people the sincerity, boldness and intelligence of leadership, and originality of action and language.

I AM that I AM is the Ineffable Name which is key to the mysteries of the universe.

And the Song of the Lamb is the second utterance of the upward-visioned among us. It is the name JESUS CHRIST. "In my Name," said He. "In His Name," said His disciples. They never preached any doctrine except the power of His Name. This was their Song. It is a Name as immaculate as the Name I AM. It always means, God with us – Emmanuel. It is that Name of the Lofty and Everlasting I AM which represents His nearness and immanence.

Class Notes

The Name JESUS CHRIST is above principalities and powers. It is the Name of newness, of healing, and of comforting tenderness. It gives the baptism of the quickening Spirit. It is the greatest and quickest God-formulating Name. It is the Name that restores the Lost Word, the now unspeakable Name of the Self-Existent Deity.

The Risen Christ, appearing suddenly, said, "Preach repentance… in My Name…. beginning at Jerusalem." (*The Self*) (Lk 24:47) Begin with yourself to repent, to return. Lift up the willing inner sight toward the Supreme One, whose Soundless Edict through the ages is, "Look unto Me, and be ye saved." (Is 45:22) Taste the first manna, which the upward watch sprinkles over the unfed brain and heart.

Let us take MONDAY to repent, or to turn away our faces from all the things, events and people that call our attention. Let us often look toward the Deity ever beholding us.

Facing toward the Heights, where the smile of the Comforting One begins its beaming Omnipresence, Omnipotence, and Omniscience speak from the heart the two greatest Names ever written or spoken on earth. They are the only response the heart can make when the mystic eye is first uplifted.

Whatever comes upon you this day, or threatens to disturb, or overthrow you at any time, turn then from it toward that High Deliverer and within the silent heart, sing the two Wonderful Songs of the Seers of the ages:

O High and Lofty One inhabiting Eternity! Clothing Thyself with Thine own Omnipresence, Omnipotence and Omniscience, as with a garment - hiding Thy goodness and majesty with names, and unspeakable names! I know Thou art, and the Name of power and glory I must address to Thee is, "I Am That I Am."

O Countenance beholding me, looking toward me through the ages! Breath of the everlasting life in me, and manna to my fadeless substance! Thy Name that folds me round with tenderness, and lifts me high above the pitfalls of my human destiny, is "Jesus Christ."

Class Notes

Chapter Two - Remission, Denial of all but God.

2nd Gate - **There is no mixture of evil in my good. There is no opposition to my God as material conditions of any kind. There is no absence of life, substance, or intelligence. There is nothing to hate. There is no presence of sin, sickness, or death in my world, where God is the only presence and power and wisdom.**

What we most often view with the inner eye, we show forth outwardly. With vision in the dust, we never feel the dissolving power of free grace. Jesus said, "Preach remission," preach the dissolving Grace.

"When men are cast down thou shall say, There is lifting up, and God shall save the humble person." (Job 22:29) There are shouts of freedom handed down from antiquity that represent the experiences of remission, or liberation of the upward watchers throughout the ages. They declare the disappearance of foolishness and ignorance.

There is no healing or illumination in descriptions of evil. The description of evil doubles evil – it does not lessen it.

According to Jesus the risen and triumphant man of God, we are to look up to the shining face of our Father looking tenderly down upon us, and declare, "Steadfastly facing Thee, there is no evil on my pathway." For only abundance and gentle kindness fall from the Vast Countenance shining toward us. "Oh, our God our eyes are upon Thee." (2 Ch 20:12)

St. Augustine found that God sees no evil. So did Habakkuk: "Thou art of purer eyes than to behold evil, and canst not look on iniquity." (Hab 1:13)

We catch the viewpoint of those with whom we associate. Let us catch the High God's viewpoint and go free from sight of evil. "Sing, O daughter of Zion; shout, O Israel; be glad and rejoice with all thy heart, O daughter of Jerusalem. The Lord hath taken away thy judgments, he hath cast out thine enemy: the king of Israel, even the Lord, is in the midst of thee: thou shalt not see evil any more!" (Zeph 3: 14-16) Zephaniah saw for a short period as his God was seeing.

Matter also has been found to have no health in its operations. No descriptions of matter quicken the pulses with healing blood, or fill the stomach with strengthening energy. No study of matter illuminates the spiritual wisdoms that wait like unlighted candles just above our heads. Only the kindling fires of God's hot Glance can illuminate our waiting intelligence. And we must recognize the Glance, acting under obedience to the order, "Behold Me." (Is 65:1)

Matter moves aside for indestructible free grace to act, when by upward viewing we shout, "Facing Thee, there is no matter with its laws."

There is no healing in descriptions of lack and deprivation. "They shall want for no good thing." (Ps 34:10. We must preach that facing the Father there is neither lack not deprivation.

There is no acting free grace visible to one who describes hurts and pains. Peter sank into the raging waters when he took his gaze off the powerful Jesus. (Mat 14) But with eyes uplifted, he walked above the waves, side by side with Omnipotence.

There is a shout of liberty any one can give when hurts come grinding and burning upon him: "Facing Thee, there is nothing to fear, for nothing shall by any means hurt me." (Luke 10:19). All hurting power is darkness. The dayspring from on high gives light to them that sit in darkness, to guide their feet into the way of peace. (Luke 1:79)

Sinfulness with its sickness and death is only the description of what is encountered by people with aberrated vision or downward gaze. It is downward gazing to describe a child's bad temper or a friend's unkindness. Not only they, but we who describe, must get warped and ill by such descriptions.

The shout of the free must be given before we feel the freedom: "Facing Thee, there is neither sin, nor sickness, nor death."

Let us take TUESDAY to shout liberty – free grace – remission – unburdening, as we look upward. Free grace comes softly stealing over the track of the upward watch. Take the shouts in order. Look at the Vast Countenance with its beaming and kindling free grace, its dissolving alkahest, ever streaming toward us.

With joyous heart proclaim:

Steadfastly facing Thee, there is no evil on my pathway.

Steadfastly facing Thee, there is no matter with its laws.

Steadfastly facing Thee, there is no loss, no lack, no absence and no deprivation.

Steadfastly facing Thee, there is nothing to fear, for there shall be no power to hurt.

Steadfastly facing Thee, there is neither sin, nor sickness, nor death…. And so it is.

Chapter Three - Forgiveness, Affirmation of all as God.

3rd Gate - **God is all. God is the Omnipresent, Omnipotent, Omniscient Good, as Life, Truth, Love, Substance, and Intelligence. I am my own idea of God. I live, and move and have my being according to my idea of God. I am spirit, mind, like my God, and shed abroad wisdom, strength, and holiness. My God works through me to will and to do that which ought to be done by me. I am governed by the True God. I am kept from sin, from suffering for sin, and I cannot fear sin, sickness, or death.**

Obedience to the mandate: "Look unto Me," introduces a new order. High watchers are enriched and set in authority from above, not by effort, not by worthiness, but by Resistless Grace. Spirit Almighty acts on our behalf.

As the needle can become a magnet by rubbing against a magnet, so we can do God-works by closely relating ourselves to the Healer of all diseases, the Redeemer from destruction, the Great in Counsel. We always become like those with whom we associate. Let us choose to be identified with the Lord, Strong and Mighty. By association with the *Alkahest* (Free Grace) its remitting absoluteness is ours. Those who communicate with me strengthen, said the Lord of Strength. Those who speak unto me waken. Those who touch me are cured. To them who hold their conversation aright will I show salvation.

As the needle must utterly yield itself so must we utterly yield ourselves. We must have our eye single to One Only to be full of the One Only. Utter yielding is called "meekness," in the Scriptures. The risen Christ taught volitional meekness, volitional offering: "He that humbleth himself shall be exalted." (Luke 14:11) He taught them to breathe in the Almighty; to wake the God-Seed by vision, by breath; for the inspiration of the Almighty awakens understanding, stirs God. "But ye shall receive power, after that the Holy Ghost is come upon you: and ye shall be witnesses unto me… unto the uttermost part of the earth." (Acts 1:8)

When the Apostles, worshippers of Almighty Sonship, preached the Risen Christ Jesus, they raised the dead and cured many taken with palsy and lameness. Volitional inspiration or breathing in of the Heavenly Breath is sure healing of the mind; sure transformation of our thinking; sure healing of the whole body; sure healing of affairs also. The healing breath never fails, never changes, abides forever in miracle-working competence, exactly as Job reported: "The breath of the Almighty hath given me life."(Job 33:4)

Class Notes

Today there are those who, by contemplating the Healing God, rather than their own pains, have been given for their diseased bodies, vigorously healthy ones. For their depressed minds, they have been given buoyancy of heart - thus bodily preaching forgiveness.

There is a ground of ready affiliation in our constitution, in which the germs of contagion find strong root – God if we contagion God; misery if we contagion misery.

"He that humbleth himself shall be exalted."(Lk 14:11, 18:14) They who let themselves go to the Finished Fact, as the inconsequent needle yields to the magnet's empowering, are new characters on the earth. By their utter meekness, they are liberated from themselves, and do the works of the Worker unto Whom they have yielded themselves.

The Sacred Books lay great stress on voluntary surrender to the Divine Trend. "Put on humbleness, meekness."(Col 3:12) "Because thine heart was tender and thou didst humble thyself before God...I will for-give ...because of meekness."(II Ch 34:27)

The Saving Sovereignty in the Universe has come to give us skill and understanding. We gladly offer the sum total of our unlikeness to the Almighty Giver, the Healing God.

Let us take WEDNESDAY to voluntarily offer ourselves to the King of Kings and Lord of Lords. They that worship in meekness are the ready harp strings for the divine melodies of the five hymns of praise – the five proclamations of truth. They are the voicing instruments of health and quickening life.

Here is a form for voluntary surrender of self in meekness:

Here is my mind; I spread it out before Thee. For-give Thou its foolishness and ignorance with Thy Bright Wisdom.

Here is my life impulsion; I offer it to Thee. For-give thou all its contrariness to Thee.

Here is my heart; it is Thine only. For-give Thou its dissatisfactions; for-give its restlessness. For-give its discouragements; for-give its elations. For-give its hopes and its fears, its loves and its hates.

Here is my body I cast it down before Thee. For-give Thou its imperfections with Thy Perfection.

For-give me altogether with Thyself.

So only can I be the life and inspiration of the five bold words of Truth.

Thou art and there is none beside Thee, in Thine own Omnipresence, Omnipotence, and Omniscience.

I am Thine only and in Thee I live, move and have my being.

I am Thine own Substance, Power and Light, and I shed abroad wisdom, strength, and holiness from Thee.

Thou art now working through me to will and to do that which ought to be done by me.

I am for-given and governed by Thee alone, and I cannot sin, I cannot suffer for sin, nor fear sin, sickness, or death.

Chapter Four - Faith, the Evidence that God is All.

4th Gate - I do believe that the true God is now working with me and through me and by me and for me, to make me a living demonstration of omnipresent, omnipotent, omniscient goodness.

As a lighted candle lights another, so conviction fires conviction. We rise up with that authority before which we have been meek. Joseph was meek in the prison house of Egypt's Pharaoh. He stopped his own thinking until the Unseen Knower touched his brain with divine wisdom and words not known by anyone on earth.

We find that the people, who have been baptized with originality, have let the world's thinking alone, and have let go even of their own thinking - so creative new knowledge has been free to touch them. This is the magic wisdom of Jesus of Nazareth: "Take no thought" – "In such an hour as ye think not."(Lk 12:40)

The world now needs fresh news from Universal Wisdom, new distillations from Divine Beneficence, sparkling gray matter drops charged with healing from on high.

Jesus discussed the mystery of forgiveness. He proved the mystery of bold use of the Working Executive facing us through all things, ever saying: "Boldly tell Me what to do and when to act."(Eph 6:20)

Deity is no disciplinarian giving us hardships, but a Beneficent Presence awaiting our use of the everywhere facing Beneficence by bold insistence

This One is no hound of heaven, hounding us to starvation, cold, or death. Neither are we His hound dogs beaten into submission to His ceaseless discipline. Let us take right view of Him: "Ask what ye will," (Jn 15:7). "Concerning the works of my hands, command ye me."(Is 45:11) "Is anything too hard for me?"(Gen 18:14) "I will work, and none shall hinder."(I Sam 14:6)

Speak boldly, looking to the face of the answering Substance, "Deliver Thou me from evil!" "Give me this day my super-substantial bread!" "Give me courage, confidence to insist! Bless me with life, wisdom, and divine efficiency!"(Matt 6: 9-13)

This recognition picks up the formulating substance and translates it into the mystic's fulfilled assurance. So shall thy life renew; so shall inspiration teach thee; so shall thy affairs go newly right with thee.

We light our inner vision by exalting it. Lightened vision wakes all our faculties to sense the Supernal Good Will surrounding us, forever wooing our positive high watch. Give me for my weakness, strength to command Thee!

Speaking boldly from my bright secret Self, I am Strength Itself – I am flawless Confidence, I am Master of the willing God of my universe. This is the "opening of the lips with right things,"(Prov 23:15) and all the divine forces stand ready to minister to my leaping Word.

The meekness of the mind, the will and the heart, opening to the Healing Good, is moving aside for a lordship not of flesh to act. "Watch therefore; for ye know not what hour," (Mat 24:42) your lordship rises.

It is the rising of the divine ego, which makes us victoriously bold. "Come boldly unto the throne," (Heb 4:16) Boldness has genius, power, and magic in it; what you can dream you can do. Therefore, be bold! Be persistent!

Though my low views have sent me loss of friends, pain and humiliation, yet truly am I a strong child of God, with dominion in all my vital sap. I am at my roots greater than my environments and the shadows of hardship with which I have darkened my path by turning from the Highest.

Omnipotence stands before me, and behind me, at my right and at my left, above me, and below me.

Is not faith the gift of God? Is not faith the confidence of things chosen according to the same high information? And does not masterfulness rise with confidence? And are we not told to have the faith, which is the masterfulness of God Himself? "Have the faith of God." (Mk 11:22)

If your eye seeks the Lord only, your whole body shall be full of wisdom. If your eye seeks the Lord only, He will fulfill your desire. If your eye seeks the Lord only, He will be your strong confidence. If your eye chooses the High Deliverer, your dominion shall rise up.

Let me not turn aside from facing Thee! Deliver Thou me from evil. Thou art empowering Obedience. I owe Thee bold command, O Thou Owner of all the kingdoms!

Jesus told his disciples to speak to the Supreme Servant in the terms of the Lord's Prayer as the firm insistence of their own lordship or 'hidden man of the heart' (1 Pet 3:4) whom all authorities obey. It is a formula full of short commands to the Great Servant who asks, "Is anything too hard for me?" (Jer 32:27)

Let us take THURSDAY, to practice speaking to the Great Servant with firm command, in the words of the hidden Lord's Formula. We will speak it over and over fifteen times. "Fifteen" is the number where the waters of misfortune cease to prevail against us. (Gen 7:20). It is the number of rising to walk above hardship.

Hallowed be Thy name.

Thy kingdom come,

Thy will be done.

Give me this day my super-substantial bread.

Forgive my debt of confidence to command Thee.

Give for my emptiness Thy substance

Let me not into temptation.

Warn me when I turn away from Thee

Deliver me from evil

Grow more and more urgent, insistent and commanding, as you go on repeating the Great Formula to the Greatest Servant among us. Let confidence solidify. Let the God-Spark speak.

"Thine, O Lord, is the greatness, and the power, and the glory, and the victory, and the majesty. For all that is in the heaven and in the earth is thine. Thine is the kingdom, O Lord, and thou art exalted as head above all. Both riches and honor come of thee, and thou reignest over all. In thine hand is power and might; and in thine hand it is to make great, and to give strength unto all. Now therefore, our God, we thank thee, and praise thy glorious name."(I Ch 29:11-13)

Class Notes

Chapter Five - Works are the rest of mind in the Presence of God

5th Gate - **As spirit, I can preach the gospel, heal the sick, cast out demons, and raise the dead.**

Confidence or faith in anything, works according to the level of confidence. Conviction is not properly speaking conviction until it turns into action. "Faith without works is dead." (Jas 2:20)

The most wonderful achievements of humankind have been brought to pass by confidence in some wonder-working Unseen Power.

There is One King of Kings and Lord of Lords, whose whole purpose toward His kingdom has ever been peace, health, wisdom and majesty. "Look unto me." (Is 45:22) "I extend peace like a river." (Is 66:12) "I am the Lord that healeth thee." (Ex 15:26) "I will instruct thee and teach thee." (Ps 32:8) These are the words of the High Redeemer inhabiting Eternity, whose way upon the earth is the saving health of the nations.

There is a science, which runs like a river of light above all the sciences. It is the Mystical Science. According to its practice, "The Lord shall fight for us and we shall hold our peace." (Ex 14:14) "All my trust on thee is stayed." (Acts 18:10) "Fear not, I will help thee." (Is 41:10) "Look onto Me." (Is 45:22)

People must learn the law of lifting up their faces to the Lord Supreme who brings noble conditions of life into view. "I will set them in order before thine eyes." (Ps 50:21) "I restore to you the years that the locust hath eaten." (Joel 2:25)

Expect greatly from above, and greatly shall restorations multiply. "Prove me now herewith, saith the Lord of hosts, if I will not pour out a blessing that there shall not be room enough to receive it." (Mal 3:10)

When our mind no longer conceives itself to be the knower, recognizing that Free Spirit is the Knower and Doer, only then we are liberated from the laws of mind and matter.

So it is that Self-recognition awakens. So is new mind built. So is hidden ability set astir. So arises the new race of which Jesus was the forerunner. Jesus stands to humankind as the embodiment of divine insistence – His name above principalities and powers, and above every name that could be named.

Jesus, the Bloom in the garden of man, came and charged Himself to become completely one with the Divine Presence in the universe. He fulfilled the prophecy of the Jews that one would come, who would be so at One with Absolute God, that He could be slain and yet not dead. One who could chemicalize out of existence, and thus make nothing all the maladies of earth.

The work of Jesus was the redemption of humankind from sin, sickness, and death, thus allowing us to walk through a redeemed world. This was His chosen work; and it is only fair for humankind to acknowledge the completeness and splendor of His finished chosen work. Jesus was charged to the supreme with Christ power.

Let us acknowledge the great and unprecedented and un-copiable achievement of Jesus of Nazareth, who by recognition of his own Soul, did the humanly impossible. He is the pivotal man. He is the Soul-bloom in the garden of man, the first fruits of them that slept. (I Cor 15:20)

We will take Friday to acknowledge before High God the surpassing accomplishment of Jesus of Nazareth. Let us acknowledge before God, that we walk through a redeemed, healed, un-punishable world, because of the vicarious suffering of Jesus of Nazareth, who being all Godhood, was forever Christ Jesus – or God Jesus – the living manifestation of what man can do and be by recognition of his own sonship to Omnipotence. "That God the Father may give you the Spirit of Wisdom and revelation for the acknowledgement of him. (Eph 1:17)

Let us accept our liberty. Let us accept our health, let us accept our redemption by stating what hath been done. So shall we by sighting one completed work enter upon our own ordained opus.

We are all posited on this planet for the one purpose of accomplishing some great opus, or work of a unique and inimitable sort. We do this by the recognition of our own divinity, our own free bold spirit, offspring of Almighty Jehovah. We have the example among the multitudinous sons of men, of One who was the first fruits of them that slept in non-recognition of their own divine equipment.

As Divine Mind, which I am, I can preach the gospel, I can heal the sick, I can cast out demons, I can raise the dead. I work the works of God, who works through me to will and to do that which ought to be done by me. I do this according to the doctrine of Jesus Christ; "The words that I speak unto you, I speak not of myself, but the Father that dwelleth in me, he doeth the works." (Jn 14:10) Thus the highest working power is to see that we have nothing to do – the Spiritual world is already perfect.

In Christ Jesus all works are finished, awaiting only acknowledgment to be plainly visible. Great signs shall follow them that believe in the redemptive labor of the Divinity-awakened Lord of Galilee. "For it is the Father's good pleasure to give you the kingdom." (Lk 12:32)

Chapter Six - Understanding of God, the only understanding worthwhile.

6th Gate - **I understand the secret of instantaneous spiritual demonstration.**

When we often give our attention to *Ain Soph*, the Great Countenance of the Absolute, we become visibly charged with newness of Divine Life. "Seek ye my face and live." (Amo 4:5) "I give life to the faint." (Is 40:29) "And I will reveal unto them the abundance of peace and truth." (Jer 33:6)

We call our relationship with the High Eternal First Cause, inspiration, because it comes along with our inward breathing. "The inspiration of the Almighty giveth them understanding." (Job 32:8). We call it Spirit, or Breath of the Almighty. Breathe toward me heavenly breath, till all this breathing form of me quickens with breath divine.

We look toward an object before thinking it. We are all harvesting according to our inward viewings. Jesus asks, "Why are ye troubled?" (Lk 24:38) Why do thoughts arise in your hearts?" (Lk 24:38)

High Mysticism is not a science of right thinking, or right conduct; these are strenuous labors. High Mysticism is the call to look up to *Ain Soph*, the Great Countenance of the Absolute, who orders thoughts and speech and conduct anew. "I will return unto that people a new language." (Zep 3:9) "They shall speak with new tongues." (Mk 16:17)

Our speech always declares the direction of our inward viewing, by the harvest of our life conditions. I we mention the shiftlessness, the sorrows, the sufferings of our neighbors, we may experience some unpleasantness of body and affairs formulated by the inward gazing our verbal descriptions betray. "Is it not written that the wages of sin (or aberrated vision) is death?" (Rom 6:23)

Mysticism is not a science of goodness and badness of conduct. It is the science of that which harvests as good or bad conduct. It is the science of the genesis of conduct and the genesis of thoughts.

Our initial and compelling faculty is our inner vision. Vision often God-ward and live anew. "So shall the body be like a tree planted by rivers of water – whose leaf fadeth

not." (Ps 1:3) Vision often God-ward so that all affairs also may go well. Gaze often toward Our Father, and all thoughts shall be like morning music. Lift up in inward look now and then, to a country whose ether winds, ever raying forth their healing aura, are swift remedies for all the world's unhappiness.

Mystical invocation is the way to know new things from the heights above the margins of the mind, where things so far untaught lie waiting our mystical invocation. "The Holy Ghost, whom the Father will send in my name, he shall teach you all things." (Jn 14:26)

Some names, especially the name Jesus Christ, are like alabaster boxes of empowering ointment. Break them open by invoking them, and mysterious new influences awake through the body, mind and environment.

Jesus, who was Christ with the fullness of the Godhead bodily, insisted that His name sheds forth fresh life: "My words are life." (Jn 6:63) "I came that you might have life." (Jn 10:10) "I am the living bread." (Jn 6:51) "He that eateth me, even he shall live by me." (Jn 6:57)

Jesus declared that His Name would stir the ether-breaths of the unseen eternal world to inbreathe with our inbreathing. There is no science of wealth or health so great as the science of volitional in-breath. Invocation is the greatest efficiency of prayer.

Upward watchers can catch heavenly health by their persistence heavenward, until their health breaks forth like the morning, and every sick person catches health from them. "I can do all things through Christ which strengtheneth me." (Phil 4:13)

Instead of much attention to material things, let us lift up our eyes to the Sender of the mystic cure and make all our draft on these immortal streams and the mysteries of health, and prosperity, and incessant renewal shall be revealed and experienced. "Whatsoever ye shall ask in my name that will I do." (Jn 14:13) "Ask what ye will, and it shall be done unto you – All things are delivered unto me of my Father." (Mat 11:27)

To be charged to overflowing with irresistible miracle-working power, while yet manifest in the flesh; to be the radiance of buoyant joy while yet walking among the children of earth. To shed the perfume of healing and strengthening and illuminating while yet speaking with us and smiling upon us is the final Christian ministry. This is the bloom of full obedience to the Sacred Edict, "Look unto Me." (Is 45:22)

There is no warfare where the vision of God is. There is no disease where the healing Name is called. There is no inadequacy or failure while the Spirit of God is in the nostrils, inbreathed as the only breath. This is Living Truth.

Let us take Saturday and Sunday to call upon the name Jesus Christ. "Far above all rule and dominion, and above every name that is named, not only in this age but also in that which is to come." (Eph 1:21) Jesus set His vision toward the Author of success, and inbreathed the airs of Paradise. He opened the gates between Himself and unstinted transcendence. Jesus rose to immortality, and His Name is full of life-giving, miracle working energy.

There is an ineffable name, the key to the mysteries of the universe. According to the Christian Scriptures, the name Jesus Christ is that revealing name, key to all understanding. Whatever we look toward, we come into identification with. Choose this day the objective of your vision: Christ Jesus..

He that seeks me identifies with me. He reigns with me. He lives as my life, he strengthens as my strength, he understands as my understanding. What I Am – he is. He calls upon my victorious Name, and whatsoever he does prospers, reminding humankind of my ever-present, ever-friendly, ever-available Supremacy. For I send the Healing Ghost, the Enwisdoming Breath to him that calls my Miracle-Working Name – Christ Jesus – bursting through which is the other Name, only known to them that invoke my Anointing Name.

Class Notes

WISEWOMAN PRESS
Books Published by WiseWoman Press

By Emma Curtis Hopkins
- *Resume*
- *The Gospel Series*
- *Class Lessons of 1888*
- *Self Treatments including The Radiant I Am*
- *High Mysticism*
- *Genesis Series 1894*
- *Esoteric Philosophy Deeper Teachings in Spiritual Science*
- *Drops of Gold Journal*
- *Judgment Series in Spiritual Science*
- *Bible Interpretations: Series I, thru XVII*

By Ruth L. Miller
- *Unveiling Your Hidden Power: Emma Curtis Hopkins' Metaphysics for the 21st Century*
- *Coming into Freedom: Emily Cady's Lessons in Truth for the 21st Century*
- *150 Years of Healing: The Founders and Science of New Thought*
- *Power Beyond Magic: Ernest Holmes Biography*
- *Power to Heal: Emma Curtis Hopkins Biography*
- *The Power of Unity: Charles Fillmore Biography*
- *Power of Thought: Phineas P. Quimby Biography*
- *The Power of Insight: Thomas Troward Biography*
- *The Power of the Self: Ralph Waldo Emerson Biography.*
- *Gracie's Adventures with God (Editor)*
- *Uncommon Prayer*
- *Spiritual Success*
- *Finding the Path*

By Frances B. Lancaster
- *The 13th Commandment*
- *Abundance Now*

By Christine Green
- *Authentic Spirituality – A Woman's Guide to Living An Empowered Life*
- *A Caregivers Journal*

By Cath DePalma
- *I Can Do This Thing Called Life And So Can You*

www.wisewomanpress.com

www.ingramcontent.com/pod-product-compliance
Lightning Source LLC
Chambersburg PA
CBHW080341170426
43194CB00014B/2651